George E. Vandeman

It Is Written Classics

TRUTH
OR
PROPAGANDA

George E. Vandeman

Pacific Press Publishing Association
Boise, Idaho
Montemorelos, Nuevo Leon, Mexico
Oshawa, Ontario, Canada

Edited by Ken McFarland
Cover design by Tim Larson
Portrait of George Vandeman by Ilyong Cha
Type set in 10/12 Century Schoolbook

First Printing 1986: 7500

ISBN 0-8163-0644-3

Contents

Section IV: My Encounter With the Claims of Christ

Before You Turn the Page

This volume, *Truth or Propaganda,* includes Pastor Vandeman's telecast scripts which search out the roots of the Christian faith. The reader will discover here a fresh and all-absorbing probe of what happened at Calvary.

The question "Does He or Doesn't He?" which introduces a series of unique science-and-Scripture telecasts, honestly explores the reasons for believing Genesis to be the authentic record of our beginnings. Pastor Vandeman's conclusions have consistently earned the respect of both reason and conscience among his many viewers and readers throughout North America, Europe, and Australia.

The third section of this volume contains a revelation. The Scripture predicts that truth—tragically lost and confused during the chaotic Dark Ages—will be rediscovered in the final hours of this world's history. Six chapters tell the story.

Then to close this compilation, Pastor Vandeman tells the exciting story of his own encounter with the claims of Christ.

The Ragtag and Bobtail

In the early days of Christianity the pagan critic Celsus jeered at Jesus. Scornfully he called Him the strangest of teachers. Why? Because "while all the others cry, 'Come to me, you who are clean and worthy,' this singular Master calls, 'Come to me, you who are down and beaten by life;' and so, being taken at his word by these impossible people, he is followed about by the ragtag and bobtail of humanity trailing behind him."

To this the Christian scholar Origen gave a devastating reply. "Yes," he said, "but he does not leave them the ragtag and bobtail of humanity; but out of material you would have thrown away as useless, he fashions men, giving them back their self-respect, enabling them to stand up on their feet and look God in the eyes. They were cowed, cringing, broken things. But the Son has made them free."

Have you ever noticed—and of course you have—that sometimes the people hardest to have around are those who have never sinned? At least they have never acknowledged any imperfection. The Bible says that "all have sinned" (Romans 3:23). But there are those who consider themselves exceptions to the rule.

People are supposed to be good. Right? Then how is it that some saints are so hard to live with? How is it that so many obviously good people seem to have been washed—but certainly not ironed? Have you ever been guilty of thinking you would rather have some terrorist as a neighbor in heaven than your Aunt Kate?

7

How is it that Jesus—though He was perfect, though He was divine—was so comfortable to be around, so easy to live with? How is it that the worst of sinners found in Him an understanding Friend? Yet the religious leaders of His day, with their rigid and picky man-made requirements, with their frowns of disapproval, made the people tense and fearful.

The answer is that Jesus loved sinners, even those whom others considered the ragtag and bobtail—the riffraff, the rabble. He ate with them, comforted them, healed them, lifted them up. The one class that He could not tolerate were those who considered themselves to be without sin. They were the ones He could never reach. He loved them, but they did not want to be loved. He wanted to save them. But they were offended by any suggestion that they needed saving.

Jesus had "not come to call the righteous, but sinners to repentance." Matthew 9:13, KJV. He had come "into the world to save sinners." 1 Timothy 1:15, KJV. And only sinners need apply!

Does all this mean that Jesus was slightly soft on sin? No. Never. It means, rather, that He had the remarkable and priceless ability to hate sin and love the sinner—at the same time. He managed to be on the side of the sinner without ever once condoning his sin.

A woman was dragged unceremoniously into His presence one day as He was teaching. She had been caught in the act of adultery, her accusers said. Should she be stoned as specified in the law of Moses? They pretended to want His counsel. But under the pretense was a carefully laid plot. If He said she *should not* be stoned, they would accuse Him of forsaking the law of Moses. And if He said she *should* be stoned, they would report Him to the Roman authorities. For the Romans, you see, didn't want the Jews playing around with capital punishment.

Jesus saw through the trap they had set. He appeared to ignore their question. He stooped down and began to write with His finger in the dust at His feet—as if He had not heard them. And this angered them. They didn't like to be ignored.

They moved closer, pressing Him for an answer. And then, looking down, they read what He was writing. And they were stunned. Could it be? Could it be that there, traced before them in the dust, were the guilty secrets of their own lives?

"All right," He challenged, "hurl the stones. But only he who has never sinned should throw the first stone!" And He went on writing.

Did Jesus know that her accusers were the very ones who had led her into sin? I believe He did. No wonder they disappeared. Fearful that the curious crowd would look over their shoulders and read what was written in the dust, they just slipped silently away, leaving the woman alone with Jesus.

Paralyzed with shame and fear, expecting that first stone to strike at any moment, she had been afraid to look up. But now she heard the gentle voice of Jesus. "Where are your accusers? Didn't even one of them condemn you?"

"No, sir," she replied.

And then came the most beautiful words she had ever heard. "Neither do I condemn you. Go and sin no more."

Jesus had the perfect opportunity to indulge in a cross examination and lecture that she would never forget. But He didn't. Rather, He sought to cover her embarrassment and her shame. He said only, "Go and sin no more." And that was enough. She knew He wasn't soft on sin. But she knew, too, that she had found an understanding Friend. Is it any wonder that she would love Him forever?

Yes, it was the hypocritical accusers, not the victim, that went away from that encounter embarrassed and licking their wounds.

Jesus had come "to heal the brokenhearted" (Luke 4:18, KJV), not to create new hurts. He was always sensitive to the feelings of others. He never needlessly embarrassed anyone or exposed a guilty one publicly. Not even Judas. Again and again He could have exposed the evil intentions of the one who would betray Him. Instead He tried to love him away from his terrible deed.

Barbara Walters was interviewing Patty Hearst for television. Patty Hearst. Kidnapped at the age of nineteen. A girl who "had never had anything bad happen" to her. Locked in a closet, blindfolded, for fifty-seven days. Tortured, interrogated, raped. Repeatedly threatened with death. Forced to rob a bank. Now a criminal wanted by the FBI. Convinced that her parents had abandoned her, that they would never have anything to do with her, that she could never go home again. Convinced that this was the end, that she was finished, that she might as well give up and join her captors. Convinced that the FBI would shoot her on sight—or if they didn't her SLA companions would. So convinced, so desperately convinced, that when she had opportunity after opportunity to escape, the thought never entered her mind to try!

Barbara Walters, excellent reporter that she is, pressed the questions closer and closer—at times almost mercilessly, it seemed. "Why didn't you give up?" "Why didn't you say, 'I don't want to make that tape'?" "Why did you behave that way?" "You had many opportunities to escape. . . . Why didn't you?" "You were alone for several days. . . . You could have picked up the phone and called your folks. Why didn't you do that?"

"It never crossed my mind."

And we can't understand. We can't understand why someone does not do what we think we would have done. We are so sure that in similar circumstances we would have grabbed a phone in seconds, or let out a bloodcurdling scream that could be heard for blocks, or raced to the nearest police officer. And we are certain that once we were free, in the friendly hands of police, we wouldn't have clenched our fists in a gesture of loyalty to the revolution and given our occupation as "urban guerrilla." It wouldn't have taken us a week to realize that we "didn't have to say those things anymore" in order to survive. We are so good at asking questions—and measuring the answers by our own "unkidnapped" thinking.

But Jesus understands. He understands the kidnap victim. He understands the sinner. He understands you and me.

Think for a moment of the embarrassing questions that Jesus could ask *us*—if He were a reporter! But He doesn't. He isn't like that!

Come with me back to the day when Jesus sat beside a well at noon—tired and thirsty. A woman came with her waterpot to draw water. And Jesus asked her for a drink.

A Jew? Asking a Samaritan for a drink? She was shocked that a Jew would even speak to her!

But Jesus knew that she was far thirstier than He. He knew that she had been drinking from polluted wells, disappointing wells. And He said to her, in a voice filled with a sympathy and tenderness she had never known, "If you knew the gift of God and who it is that asks you for a drink, you would have asked him and he would have given you living water." John 4:10, NIV.

She wanted that living water. And Jesus told her to go and call her husband and come back.

"I have no husband," she replied. And Jesus told her that she had had five husbands, and that the man with whom she was now living was not her husband.

Startled, she tried to change the subject. And who wouldn't? For she realized that she was in the presence of One who knew everything about her. Yet He still wanted to give her living water. Could He possibly be the promised Messiah? And Jesus told her, "I who speak to you am he." Verse 26, NIV.

She was so excited that she forgot her waterpot, forgot to give Jesus a drink, and rushed back to the city, telling everyone she met, "Come, see a man who told me everything I ever did. Could this be the Christ?" Verse 29, NIV.

Jesus had told her to call her husband, but she called everybody she knew. The Saviour looked out across the fields and there they came! The plumber. The ditchdigger. The banker. The landlord. The tenant. The doctor. The neighbor. The friend. The uncle. The brother-in-law. The fields were white with the robes of Samaritans coming to see a Man. And Jesus was glad. Because He knew how much they needed living water!

What a lecture Jesus could have given to a woman with a past like hers! What scathing denunciations could have fallen from His lips! He could have pressed the embarrassing questions mercilessly. But no one would have come back across the fields to see the Man!

Friend, I want to echo the words of that Samaritan woman, "Come, see a Man! Leave your disappointing wells that never satisfy. Stop trying to dig your own wells. Digging is thirsty work. Come and meet Jesus. Come and drink. And you need never thirst again!"

San Francisco and the East Bay were in the grip of a heat wave. And it was camp meeting time. In those days everyone lived and cooked and slept in tents at camp meeting. And tents were stifling in the heat. Even so, the campers had crowded into the big pavilion to hear one of their favorite speakers— Pastor Luther Warren. Among them was a mother with two small children. And of course they were restless.

Finally the charming little two-year-old fell asleep in her mother's arms. The older child was blue-eyed with slightly curling blond hair. The mother was eager to hear the message and tried patiently to help the child at her side sit quietly. But it was so hot, and the folding chair was so hard. Soon came the inevitable request—a drink of water.

The mother waited, reluctant to disturb the sleeping child. Then suddenly the little girl pointed vaguely in some direction. "There's a man over there who has a drink of water!"

In those days it was not dangerous for a child to ask a stranger for a drink—especially at camp meeting. The mother gave her permission, telling the little girl to be sure to come back right away. Then she settled back and relaxed. Maybe now she could listen to the message.

Suddenly, with unbelieving eyes, she saw her small daughter walk right up on the platform and ask the speaker for a drink! She sat transfixed as she saw Pastor Warren stop and pour a glass of cold water from the pitcher that had been placed on the desk. And the child expressed her thanks by lifting her blue eyes to gaze into his.

If you ever knew Luther Warren, you would know that he didn't mind the interruption a bit. Instead, it gave him the perfect opportunity to talk about cool, invigorating, living water— on a hot, thirsty day.

Look, friend! There's a Man over there on that cross who has a drink of water! Living water! And you can walk right up to Him and ask Him for a drink. He won't mind being interrupted!

Jesus was dying that Friday afternoon. The guilt of the world's sin was crushing out His life. In all history there had never been a more important moment. And the thief on the cross beside Him interrupted His dying with a request.

What happened? The whole plan of salvation stopped and waited while Jesus answered the prayer of the repentant thief!

He will stop to answer *you*—any time! You can walk right up and ask Him for a drink—and never thirst again! You can ask Him now!

The Foolishness of Golgotha

God has some strange ways of doing things. His ways of fighting wars, of resolving conflicts, seem peculiar, even bizarre. There isn't an army general alive who would approve His strategy.

Imagine, if you can, that you are a watchman atop the wall of the ancient city of Jericho. And one day an army of 600,000 ex-slaves approaches. You smile at the idea of Jericho ever falling into *their* hands. This is going to be interesting!

So what happens? A strange procession begins to circle the city. First a company of selected warriors. Then seven priests with trumpets. Next priests in their sacred dress, bearing on their shoulders a golden chest. Then the entire army of Israel. See Joshua 6.

There is no sound except the mighty tread of marching feet—and the solemn peal of the trumpets, echoing among the hills and sounding through the streets of Jericho. Once around the city, and the army returns silently to their tents. What is going on?

The same thing happens the next day, and the next. There is something mysterious about this, something even terrifying. What can it mean? You remember that the Red Sea parted before these people and that a passage has just been made for them through the Jordan River at flood stage. And the Jordan is too close for comfort. What might the God of the Hebrews do next?

For six days a single circuit of the city is made once each day.

15

Nothing more. On the morning of the seventh day of the siege something happens that is strange and foreboding. The army does not withdraw after a single circuit of the city. It continues a second time around, and a third, and a fourth. Six times around. What will happen now? What mighty event is impending?

You have not long to wait. As the seventh circuit of the city is completed, the army pauses. The trumpets have been silent for a time, but now they break forth in a blast that shakes the very earth. The walls, with their massive towers, teeter and heave, and crash to the earth. And you can be glad that you were atop that wall only in imagination!

What a way to take a city! What a seemingly ridiculous way! Just march around it and blow trumpets! But it worked!

In the days of Jehoshaphat, king of Judah, something equally strange happened. His country was invaded by an army that would make anyone tremble. But the king, with God's encouragement, put a band of singers at the head of his army, and sent them out praising God for victory!

Who ever heard of sending a choir out at the head of the army? Isn't that a little too much? But again, it worked! When the invaders heard the singers claiming victory, they were so frightened and confused that they simply turned on each other, destroying themselves!

Then there was Gideon. He had an army of 32,000 men. God told him that was too many. So Gideon kept sending men home till he had only 300 left. These 300, at God's direction, were divided into three companies. Each man was given a trumpet and also a torch which was concealed in an earthen pitcher. The three companies approached the enemy camp from different directions. In the dead of night, on signal from Gideon's war horn, every trumpet was sounded. And then, breaking their pitchers so that the blazing torches were displayed, they rushed upon the enemy with the cry, "The sword of the Lord, and of Gideon!"

Suddenly roused from sleep, the enemy soldiers saw flaming torches on every side. From every direction came the sound of the trumpets and the cry of Gideon's men. Thinking they were being attacked by an overwhelming force, the Midianites became panic-stricken. Fleeing for their lives, they mistook their own countrymen for enemies and destroyed one another!

What strange ways of fighting! Blowing trumpets! Breaking pitchers! Shouting!

Why such unconventional methods? We find the answer in the directions God gave to Gideon. Listen: "And the Lord said to Gideon, 'The people who are with you are too many for Me to give Midian into their hands, lest Israel become boastful, saying, "My own power has delivered me."'" Judges 7:2, NASB.

Do you see? God works in ways so simple, so seemingly ridiculous, so lacking in potential, so unlikely to produce results— He does this so that we can never say, We did it ourselves!

Yes, again and again it has happened. Time after time, by doing that which appeared not very smart, God has made it plain that there is no way man could have done it. He Himself has been at work!

So when God, back in eternity, was confronted with the greatest crisis of all—the entrance of sin into His perfect universe—it is no wonder that He did not meet it in the way we might expect.

Here was a conflict involving not a single world, but the entire universe. God's character had been called in question. God Himself was on trial. His government had been challenged. The fate of all God's creation was at stake!

How would God respond? With massive force? With His superior power? Would He extinguish rebellion with one great mushroom cloud? No. God made His decision. *He would fight rebellion with a cross!*

A strange plan? Yes. And some have called it foolish!

This Jesus, from the day He arrived on this planet, seemed to violate all the rules of getting ahead. Born in a manger. Brought up in poverty. He never wrote a book. He never led an army or a protest march or a revolt or a revolution. He never enrolled in the schools considered best. He was forever at odds with the doctors of religion. He bypassed the students of Plato and Aristotle and selected uneducated fishermen as His helpers, choosing "the foolish things of the world to confound the wise; and . . . the weak things of the world to confound the things which are mighty." 1 Corinthians 1:27, KJV.

Jesus could have led a revolt against Rome. Such a move would have meant instant popularity with those who instead became His enemies. With His power to work miracles Rome wouldn't have had a chance. And think of the advantage to an army led by One who could feed all His soldiers with a little boy's lunch!

He could easily have taken the throne of David—if He had played it right. But He seemed to miss all the cues. He appeared to have no sense of timing. When the tide of public opinion had turned His way and the people were ready to make Him king, He sent the crowd home and went off into the mountain to pray. Judas was not the only one who thought He would have to get His cues better than that!

The hopes of His followers reached a peak once more on the Sunday He rode triumphantly into Jerusalem, accompanied by the waving of palm branches and the shouting of His praise. Surely He was about to assume power!

But only days later He let His enemies lead Him out of the city to a place called Golgotha. He let them put Him on a rough, splintery cross without a word of protest—and prayed for those who drove the spikes into His hands.

Not one in that crowd knew what was happening that day. Not His enemies. Not His friends—especially His friends. They knew He could deliver Himself from His enemies. They had seen Him do it before. They knew He could come down from the cross at any moment, if He chose. Why didn't He? Why was He letting Himself die? They couldn't understand.

Little did they know that what was happening was not accident. Little did they know that Jesus, according to plan, was dying in man's place. He was dying the death that sinners who reject His sacrifice must finally die. And that is not the ordinary death we all must die. It is not the death of one surrounded by friends and loved ones in his final hours. It is not the death of one attended by nurses who hold a glass of cold water to his parched lips. It is not the death of a martyr who looks into heaven as Stephen did and sees the Saviour standing over him in sympathy and love. It is not the death of the Christian who is sustained by the hope of the resurrection. In the death we are talking about there is total, complete, and final separation from God!

Jesus, there on the cross, His agony mercifully veiled by darkness, was dying the death that sinners must die. He was experiencing a rendezvous with the terrors of hell itself!

What do I mean? Simply this. Hell, when it happens, will be very, very real. The flames will be hot. But the flames will not be the worst of it. Hell's worst terror will be in the hours that precede the fire. It is knowing that the decisions of this life have been final, that it is too late to reverse them. It is seeing the glory of the City of God—and being forever shut out. It is the awful realization of what might have been, but now can never be. It is the terror of separation from God, separation from the Source of life. It is a death that will have no morning. The flames will be a quick and merciful end to the terrors of hell.

But did Jesus experience all this? Didn't He know all the time that He would be resurrected?

No. Not all the time. It is true that on several occasions He had said He would rise again. He knew it then. But that was while He was sustained by His Father's presence. As He hung there in the darkness that Friday, His Father's presence had been completely withdrawn. Not because the Father didn't care. The Father, unseen, was suffering along with His Son. But Jesus was bearing the crushing, stifling guilt of all the world. He who had no sin of His own had identified Himself with our sins, with everybody's sins, as if they were His. And there must be a gulf between God and sin. The sinner, dying his final death, will not be sustained by the Father's presence. Nor could Jesus, dying in our place. He must die alone.

The sinner must die without hope of living again. So must Jesus. He must experience that too. And He did. For as His Father's presence was completely withdrawn, He was seized by the fear that sin, the sin He was bearing for others, might be so offensive to His Father that the separation would be eternal. In those awful moments He could see no light beyond the tomb!

All the while Satan was whispering his vicious temptations with hypocritical sympathy. "You'll never see Your Father again! No one will be saved. You've wasted all these years. Even Your friends have forsaken You. Why don't You let men pay for their own sins?"

Every labored breath was drawing the Saviour nearer to what He thought might be eternal death. But He never wavered in His decision. He was willing to stay in the tomb forever—if only one, if only *you*, could be saved. That's how much He cared!

So fierce was the battle that Jesus was hardly aware of what was going on below the cross. His tormentors were looking on in compassionless scorn, and saying, "He saved others; himself he cannot save." Matthew 27:42. And Roman soldiers were playing their games of dice, unaware that the contest of the ages was going on above them.

That contest was decided not in the light of His Father's presence and approval, but in the long shadow of death—a shadow His eye could not penetrate, until the very last. It was only in His final moments that His faith broke through the darkness and He knew that He had won. Studdert-Kennedy said it so well!

> And sitting down they watched Him there,
> The soldiers did.
> There, while they played with dice,
> He made His sacrifice,
> And died upon the cross to rid
> God's world of sin.
>
> He was a gambler, too, my Christ.
> He took His life and threw
> It for a world redeemed.
> And ere His agony was done,
> Before the westering sun went down,
> Crowning that day with crimson crown,
> He knew that He had won!

Yes, what happened that day at Golgotha looked like foolishness to ambitious men. The apostle Paul would say, "We preach Christ crucified, unto the Jews a stumblingblock, and unto the Greeks foolishness." 1 Corinthians 1:23.

The foolishness of Golgotha. Sheer nonsense to those who do not understand. But God knew what He was doing. What appeared to be a terrible mistake was the most brilliant move Love could make. And what looked like ignominious defeat turned out to be Love's finest hour!

Identity Crisis

The story is told of an airline pilot assigned to international flights. Since he had several days off between work assignments, he had time for other interests and purchased a small service station.

One day, in need of some small item, he dropped in at the hardware store up the street. His purchase made, he stopped to chat about something of interest on his last flight overseas.

When he had gone, another customer asked, "Who is that man?"

And the owner replied, "Oh, he has a service station down the street here." And then with a smile, "He thinks he's an airline pilot!"

Most of us have only indulgent smiles and little compassion for the man who is confused about his own identity. We put him in what we consider to be an appropriate pigeonhole, along with the man who thinks he's Napoleon, and go on our way. But sometimes we are the ones confused, and we make some embarrassing mistakes.

It was no different in the days of Jesus. Some thought *He* was confused. Others wrote Him off as an impostor, even a blasphemer—for Jesus did claim to be God. But the matter of His true identity refused to be put to rest. For what if He was telling the truth? What if He really was God? Even His enemies could not quiet the conviction that it was they who were wrong. And it haunted them.

They asked Him right out one day, "Who are you, anyway?"

And Jesus said, "When you have lifted up the Son of Man, then you will know who I am." John 8:28, NIV.

"When you have lifted Me up. When you have crucified Me. When you have scorned Me and mocked Me and laughed at Me. When you have driven spikes into My hands. When you have hung Me between heaven and earth on a despised Roman cross and dared Me to come down if I could. When you have left Me to die without even a drink of cold water. *Then* you will know who I am!"

There He was—alone—dying. Once—yes, twice—a Voice from heaven had acknowledged Him as His Son. But now there was no voice. All was silent—except for the taunts of the mob and the angry sounds of an offended creation. Who was this Man, this compassionate Healer, this beloved Teacher? What had He done that Heaven now refused to defend Him? What crime was His that even nature was punishing Him with its fiery darts? Who was He, anyway?

Was this a man—just a good man—the best man who ever lived—dying as a passive victim in the hands of wicked men? Or was it incarnate God paying the price for a lost race in the balance?

Never forget it! If He was only a man, we are describing murder. If He was God, we are describing an offering. If He was only a man, we are witnessing a martyr. If He was God, we are witnessing a Sacrifice!

The thief on the cross beside Him knew who He was. He knew that his own moments of grace were fast slipping away. And he broke the awesome silence with the prayer, "Lord, remember me when You come into Your kingdom!"

Jesus was busy dying. Would He have any word for a thief who was dying too? Time seemed to stand still as heaven and earth waited for the Saviour's reply. "I say unto you today— today when all have forsaken Me, today when it looks as if I shall never have a kingdom—I say unto you today, You will be with Me in paradise."

The Roman centurion knew who He was. He sensed that this was no ordinary crucifixion. And when Jesus had breathed His last tortured breath, he said with conviction, caring not for the scoffing crowd, "Surely this was the Son of God!"

The enemies of Jesus knew more than they wished they knew. They had prodded Him to tell them who He was—not because they wanted to know, but because they wanted to trap Him. They desired only to be rid of Him. They couldn't bear the presence of One so pure, so untainted that their own hypocritical characters looked blacker than black. Jesus must go!

But when they had killed Him, when they had accomplished their foul deed, satisfaction escaped them. Their crime brought no sweetness at the end of the day. They feared the dead Christ more than the living Christ!

The haughty Caiaphas knew who He was. He had demanded of Jesus, "Tell us if you are the Christ, the Son of God." And Jesus had told him plainly, "Yes, it is as you say." No wonder the wily ruler would turn pale as death when he learned from the Roman guard that Jesus had walked out of the tomb!

And Pilate knew. He found no fault in Jesus. He longed to save Him from His conspiring enemies. He tried to wash the guilt from his hands. But he couldn't. To the day of his death he would live in fear of the One he ordered scourged and sent off to be crucified. Even in the supposed security of the palace, how could he be sure that the risen Jesus would not suddenly confront him and demand a reckoning?

Yes, they had prodded Him—"Who are You, anyway?" And Jesus had told them, "When you have lifted Me up, then you will know who I am."

Among those who watched Him die that dark Friday were some who never slept till they had determined from the Scriptures who He was. And many a conscience was tortured with guilt—the guilt of having joined the cruel cry of the crowd, "Crucify Him! Crucify Him!"

Picture it if you can—a man caught up in the crowd, a man who has watched about the cross, a man who has seen and heard strange things that day—frightening things.

The crowd has dispersed now, and he makes his way home alone. His accusing conscience is haunting him. Why has he done what he did? Why did he allow himself to join the crazed mob in calling for the death of a Man who has done him no wrong—a Man whom Pilate declared to be innocent? He hopes to find peace, relief from his guilt, within the walls of home. But what happens when he steps across his own threshold? The poet tells it:

> His son—the idol of his heart—lies ill.
> They weep beside his bed.
> One hope is left—the Man of Nazareth will heal.
> They know not He is dead!
>
> His son's parched lips—he sees them moving now,
> "Please take me right away."
> How can he tell him—cold and guilty words—
> "I crucified Him, son, today!"

Fifty long days passed. Truth and rumor, side by side, passed through the land—adding to, or detracting from the turmoil in the hearts of men. One question, above every other, demanded to be settled—*the identity of Jesus of Nazareth, Jesus the Crucified.*

Then came Pentecost. And Peter stood up to speak. Peter, the disciple who had run away. Peter who swore he didn't know Jesus. Peter who cursed rather than be identified with Him.

But something has happened to Peter. Boldly, without fear, and with the enemies of Jesus listening, He says, "Therefore let all Israel be assured of this: God has made this Jesus, whom you crucified, both Lord and Christ." Acts 2:36, NIV.

Think of it! What fearlessness! "This Jesus, whom you crucified! The One you crucified is the Son of God!"

And what happened? How did the crowd respond? Did they turn upon Peter? No. "When the people heard this, they were cut to the heart and said to Peter and the other apostles, 'Brothers, what shall we do?' "

Three thousand were converted that day. Three thousand fell at the feet of the Crucified One and found healing for their guilt!

"This Jesus, whom you crucified." This was the message of the early church. This was its power!

We say, We didn't do it. We didn't crucify Him. It was Pilate who did it. It was Judas. It was the Roman soldiers. We weren't there. We are not to blame!

But Jesus didn't die from nail wounds. It wasn't the pain of the spikes that killed Him. He died of a broken heart—from the weight of the sins that He carried with Him to the cross.

And listen! If our sins—yours and mine—weren't included, if it was not our sins, too, that crushed out His life, then how can we say that Jesus paid the penalty for our sins? And if they *were* included, then you and I are guilty, too, of crucifying Jesus. Our fingerprints are on the nails!

Cyril J. Davey tells the story of Sundar Singh, a boy of India. He was almost fourteen when his mother died and his world collapsed. He was desolate. No one could comfort him. He knew he could not live without God. But it seemed to him that God had taken away the only person who could ever make Him real.

Sundar attended a Christian mission school—because the government school was too far away. He had always been a quiet and courteous student. But now everything changed. Now, in his grief, he became a violent young ruffian. The kindness of the teachers only infuriated him. He hated them. He hated their school. He hated their Book. And he hated their Jesus!

One day he approached one of his teachers and politely asked to buy a New Testament. Little did anyone suspect why he wanted it.

Soon he was saying to his young friends, "Come with me. You are surprised that I should buy this Book. But come home and see what I do with it! How long I shall live I cannot tell you. Not long, certainly. But before I die I will show you what I think of Jesus and His Book!"

He led the way to the courtyard of his home, brought a bundle of sticks and a tin of kerosene, and set the wood burning. Then, slowly and methodically, he tore the pages from the Book one at a time and threw them on the fire. He wanted it to be his last gesture of contempt for the Christians' Book!

Suddenly his father walked out of the house and thundered, "Are you mad, child? Are you beside yourself to burn the

Christians' Book? It is a good Book—your mother has said so. And I will not have this evildoing in my house. Stop it! Do you hear? *Stop it!*"

Sundar bent down, stamped the rest of the New Testament into the flames with his foot, and went to his room without a word. He stayed there for three days and nights.

Then came the night that was to decide it all. He knew what he would do. Not far away he heard the sound of a train as it rushed toward Lahore and was gone. The next express would be at five o'clock in the morning. And if God had not spoken to him before then, he would go out and lay his head on the rails and wait for the train from Ludhiana to Lahore to end his miserable existence.

His mind must be clear this night. He went to the bathhouse and bathed in cold water for an hour before returning to his room. It was seven hours till the express would come through.

He prayed, "Oh God—if there be a God—reveal Thyself to me before I die!"

The hours passed.

At fifteen minutes to five he rushed into his father's room and grabbed the sleeping man by the shoulder. He burst out, "I have seen Jesus!"

"You're dreaming, child," his father said. "Go back to bed."

But Sundar was not dreaming. He told how he had planned to end his life—and rushed on with his story.

"A few minutes ago," he said, "Jesus came into my room. . . . And He spoke to me. . . . He said, 'How long will you persecute Me? I have come to save you. You are praying to know the right way. Why do you not take it? I am the Way.' "

Sundar went on. "He spoke in Hindustani, and He spoke to *me*. I fell at His feet. How long I knelt I cannot say. But when I rose the vision faded. It *was* a vision. It was no thought of mine that called Him there. . . . Had it been Krishna, or one of my own gods, I might have expected it. But not Jesus!"

He paused a moment, and spoke again. "I am a Christian. I can serve no one else but Jesus!"

His father spoke sharply, "You *must* be mad. You come in the middle of the night and say you are a Christian. And yet it is not three days past that you burned the Christians' Book!"

Sundar stood rigid, looking at his hands. And then he said with deep feeling, *"These hands did it. I can never cleanse them of that sin until the day I die!"*

No wonder he loved Jesus! No wonder he preached Jesus till the day of his death! No wonder he made his way, almost every summer, into the forbidden land of Tibet, enduring the cruelest persecution. But the more he was persecuted, the happier he was that he could suffer for his Lord. From his last trip into Tibet, he never returned!

Friend, look at your hands, as I look at mine. These are the hands that crucified Jesus! And nothing but the red, red blood of Calvary can ever make them clean!

Here is an identity crisis that must be settled by every one of us. We need to stay with it until we know who we are—and who we are not. Are we innocent bystanders, safely separated from Calvary's guilt by two thousand years? Or are we, too, the ones who crucified our Lord? When we have looked long and honestly at the cross, we will know!

But there is hope! For when Jesus prayed, "Father, forgive them," I know He meant me! I know He meant you!

What Really Happened at Calvary?

We are a generation obsessed with investigations. An airliner crashes. And even before the survivors are rescued or the fatalities counted, we launch an investigation of all available facts concerning the accident. Before a highrise fire is out, we are searching for the cause.

When a public figure is assassinated or dies under mysterious circumstances, our probing of the facts is long and thorough. Many years later some are still investigating the assassination of John F. Kennedy. Millions are not satisfied yet that we know the truth. Questions are still raised about the death of Robert Kennedy in a Los Angeles hotel just at the height of his popularity. And the full extent of responsibility for the slaying of Martin Luther King is, in many minds, a matter not completely settled.

And it is good to have an inquiring mind. It is not always wise to accept the first answer that surfaces. But have you ever really investigated the death of Jesus of Nazareth? Without question it was the most mysterious death of all time. Yet it remains a mystery only casually probed. Why? Would you like to know the inside story?

Millions of pages have been written about the death of Jesus of Nazareth, and uncounted assumptions have been made. But many of us haven't the foggiest notion of what really happened that Friday in A.D. 31 on a hill outside Jerusalem. Why has not some credible investigation ever been launched—and the facts made known? Why has so much been assumed—and so little known for sure?

Was the death of Jesus an accident? Or was it planned? And if so, by whom? Why did He die? Was His death the greatest tragedy ever to involve this planet? Or was it a victory so tremendous, so complete, that it set angels singing—and spelled doom for death itself?

Could it be that the death of Jesus has startling implications for you—implications of which you have never dreamed?

Calvary was like a giant billboard proclaiming to all who passed by that Jesus had failed. Whatever His mission—whatever He had hoped to accomplish—it had misfired. Jesus lay dead in Joseph's new tomb. And His enemies, visible and invisible, were determined to keep Him there forever!

The disciples of Jesus, till the last, had not believed He would die. He was the Messiah. And the Messiah would not die, could not die. They had expected Him to work some miracle to save Himself from His enemies. But there had been no miracle. Jesus was dead. And as they carried His lifeless body into Joseph's tomb and left it there, their spirits plummeted into deep depression.

Hear them reasoning, "We trusted that it had been he which should have redeemed Israel." Luke 24:21, KJV. But now it seemed they had made a terrible mistake. Jesus must not be the long-awaited Saviour after all. Life seemed empty and pointless. And as the sun dipped low in the western sky, reminding them that the Sabbath was about to begin, they went into hiding, fearing that they themselves might now be on the hit list of the enemies of Jesus.

Twenty-four hours later, as the sun again dropped low in the west, signaling now the end of the Sabbath, Joseph's tomb was secured by the Roman seal, with a guard of one hundred soldiers stationed close by. Jesus was locked in His rock prison as securely as if He were to remain there till the end of time.

The long night passed slowly as the soldiers kept their careful watch. A great company of angels, unseen, waited to welcome Jesus. Satan was there, for his only hope was to keep Jesus forever in the tomb. And the host of his evil angels was there too, instructed not to give ground whatever might happen.

Suddenly the angel Gabriel, the powerful angel who evidently took Lucifer's place, flew swiftly toward the earth. The planet trembled at his approach, and the evil angels scattered in terror. The Roman soldiers, petrified with fear, saw Gabriel remove the huge stone at the door of the tomb as if it were a pebble. They heard him cry, "Son of God, come forth! Your Father calls You!"

They saw Jesus walk out of the broken tomb and proclaim over it, "I am the resurrection and the life!" And they saw the angels bow low in adoration, welcoming their loved Commander with songs of praise. The soldiers heard and saw it all. And no bribe could keep them from telling it! Not now!

Yes, the cross of Calvary, that dark Friday, had stood like a giant billboard of defeat. But now Jesus of Nazareth had walked out of the tomb with the tread of a Conqueror. He had conquered death!

Jesus had not failed at all! He had accomplished His mission in every detail. But not even His own disciples understood what His mission was. He had not come to challenge Rome. He had not come to take the throne of David. He was a Man born to be crucified. He was the Lamb of God who had come to take away the sin of the world. He had come to take our sins upon Himself and die in our place, so that we could be forgiven, so that we could live. His death was not a defeat. The moment of His death marked a victory so great that it must have set the angels of heaven singing. Jesus had won!

You see, Calvary was a battlefield. It was the scene of the most crucial, the most critical, the most decisive showdown in the controversy between Christ and Satan—a controversy that began in heaven and today is moving toward its final windup. It is only in the setting of that controversy that we can begin to comprehend what really happened at Calvary. In fact, to understand that controversy is to understand the Bible. For the Bible is the story of that ongoing conflict—the story of God's plan to save men, and Satan's attempt to thwart it.

We stand in wonder at the incredible love displayed on that

old rugged cross. The God-Man dying in our place. How could we live without forgiveness? We thank God that we have a risen Saviour. We rejoice that He has conquered death, that we can look forward to a resurrection morning when loved ones will be reunited, never to part again.

All this we see in that memorable weekend. *But there is more. So much more!*

What did Jesus mean when, in the last moment before He bowed His head and died—what did He mean when He cried out, "It is finished!"? Here was not the feeble groan of a sufferer. It was the cry of a Conqueror. The words were spoken in clear, trumpetlike tones that seemed to resound through creation. What did He mean? What was finished? Why had Jesus come to this planet? What was involved in His mission? Why did He have to die to save men? Was there no other way? Did His mission, and His death, involve only fallen men? Or other worlds too?

Jesus had come to earth, and He had died, to silence the charges of Satan concerning the character of God. The rebel chief had charged that God was a harsh, tyrannical Ruler who had no real love for His subjects. He claimed that he, Satan, was the only one who cared!

But you have only to look at Calvary to see who it is that cared! That cross is the ultimate demonstration of caring. And it is a demonstration that has not been lost on the watching worlds!

Jesus had come to unmask Satan before all the universe, to let the angels and the unfallen worlds see how deadly, how lethal, how ruthless sin is—to let them see how far sin would go. When the rebellion began, it had seemed incredible that something called sin could be as dangerous as God said it was.

But as they watched through the centuries, as they saw the fallen angel spreading war and destruction everywhere, leaving a trail of heartache and pain and death, they began to understand. And when they saw Satan placing his own Creator on that despised cross, there was not a trace of sympathy left for him anywhere in the universe—except on this planet.

Jesus had come to honor His Father's law, even at the cost of

His own lifeblood. From the very beginning of the controversy between Christ and Satan, God's law had been the key issue. It was the issue that divided heaven. It was the issue in Eden. His first encounter on this planet was a shameless, brazen invitation to disobey God.

In the final crisis, just ahead of us, the issue will still be the law of God and its authority. For in the book of Revelation we see Satan, in these last days, angry, making war with those who keep the commands of God. "Then the dragon was enraged at the woman [the church] and went off to make war against the rest of her offspring—those who obey God's commandments and hold to the testimony of Jesus." Revelation 12:17, NIV.

Why did Jesus have to die to save men? Was there no other way? No. God's law had been broken, and the penalty was death. Someone must die.

My friend Lew Walton, a practicing attorney, has said it so well:

"The Creator was between the horns of a terrible dilemma, between His love for man and His love for truth.

"The entire universe depended upon a law He Himself had written, by which everything from worlds to atoms moved in order—a perfect law—and how does one change perfection? If He bent the divine law to accommodate even one small human challenge, He would be saying that perfection can be altered—and He would be following Lucifer straight into the valley of doom where there are no absolutes except one's own shifting wants."

Well said, wouldn't you say?

Could not the law be set aside, disregarded—just once? No. The law is the foundation of God's government. To play games with divine law is to invite chaos. Without law, the universe itself would fall.

Could not the law be altered just a little—to save Jesus? No. The law is a perfect transcript of the perfect character of God. He could not change His law without changing His character. He is a God of love. His law is a law of love. It defines how love will act.

The fact that Jesus did die on Golgotha's cross, in spite of its terrible cost, in spite of the incredible horror of the ordeal through which He personally must pass—here is mighty evidence, unanswerable evidence, that the law could not be changed—even to spare God's own Son. If the law could have been changed or altered or disregarded or set aside or ignored or bypassed, then the death of Jesus was unnecessary—and Calvary was only a meaningless drama!

Jesus came to demonstrate that it was possible for men to keep God's law. Satan had charged otherwise. Wasn't Adam's fall the proof? But Jesus took humanity, not in the strength of Adam, not in the perfect environment of Eden—He took humanity after it had been weakened by thousands of years of rebellion. For thirty-three years He lived just as we have to live, using no power that is not available to us—and never once sinned. And this in spite of every hellish scheme Satan could think of to trip Him up!

Jesus died to make the universe, all of it, forever secure. Rebellion *must not* happen again. And the prophet says it *will not.* "Affliction shall not rise up the second time." Nahum 1:9, KJV.

Thank God, the dreadful demonstration of sin's lethal nature will never need to be repeated! Why? Will God take away our power to choose and make us robots after all, so that we cannot sin? No. We will have seen enough of sin—at Calvary. And we shall never want to touch it again!

Jesus died to make the whole universe safe. Calvary is for other worlds too—not just for us. The unfallen worlds will be safe from rebellion through unending ages. And heaven will be safe. Not because of law. Not because of fear. But because what happened that day on a cross outside Jerusalem, as they watched in breathless horror, has made them safe!

A little boy—just a toddler—was restless one evening. He wanted to play. He wandered into his parents' bedroom and pulled open the drawer in the nightstand. He found there a shiny black pistol. It looked just like his own—the one he played with.

He carried it out to the living room, pointed it at his father, and said, "Bang, bang, Daddy! You're dead!" And his father fell to the floor. Then he pointed it at his mother and said, "Bang,

bang, Mommie! You're dead." And she fell to the floor. Just the way they had always played.

But they didn't get up, and he didn't know what to make of it. Something must be wrong. He threw the pistol away—as far as he could throw it—and knelt beside his father. "Get up, Daddy! Get up! I don't want to play anymore!"

Oh friend! Do you see what sin has done to the Saviour? Do you see what it has done to this once-beautiful world? Do you see what it has done to those you love? Do you see what it has done to you?

What else can you do but throw sin as far as you can throw it and kneel at the Saviour's feet? What can you do but let the tears roll down your cheeks unchecked and tell Him you don't want to play with sin anymore?

That's what He's been waiting for—all these years! And that's what you've been waiting for! Isn't it?

The Repainting of Golgotha

The Battle of Kadesh was reported by Ramses II, of Egypt, as only a skirmish in which he, of course, was victorious. But Ramses was a vain fellow. The Battle of Kadesh turned out to be not a skirmish at all, but one of the significant battles of history. And Ramses, rather than being the victor, barely escaped with his life.

On the massive pillars and palace walls of mighty Karnak, Ramses described again and again his conflicts with the king of Hatti. The Assyrians also frequently mentioned the land of Hatti. But historians did not guess the truth. It was assumed that the Hatti were only some unimportant tribe. No one thought to ask how an unimportant tribe could skirmish with two great powers—and for so long a time. The Hatti turned out to be not a tribe at all, but a third giant empire of that day—the Hittites, with their borders stretching from the Black Sea to Damascus.

But no matter, Ramses felt quite capable of handling the Hittites. At least he must be given credit for putting on a bold front.

One of the Egyptian inscriptions concerning the Battle of Kadesh described Ramses as the "fearless one" who "put an end to the boastfulness of the land of Hatti." He was "the son of Re who trampled the land of Hatti underfoot.... He was like a bull with sharp horns . . . the mighty lion . . . the jackal who in a moment traverses the circuit of the earth . . . the divine, splendid falcon." There was also a long poem describing the tremendous victory of Ramses.

Today it is known that these claims were shameless propaganda. Yet it was believed for more than three thousand years!

The truth is that Ramses allowed himself to be taken in by the story of two Bedouin spies sent into his camp by the Hittite king. These men, claiming to be deserters from the Hittite army, told Ramses that the Hittite king had already retreated from him in fear. And susceptible as he was to flattery, he allowed his army to fall into the trap, escaping only with his life.

A neat trick, isn't it? Lose the battle, but convince the world you won it. And succeed for three thousand years. I'm not sure who thought of such a strategy first. But there's a parallel here that I can't escape. The Battle of Kadesh was fought about 1300 B.C. but about A.D. 31 the chief of the fallen angels—we call him Satan—set out to try the same strategy. He had lost a battle infinitely more important than Kadesh. And it could be said of him, too, that he barely escaped with his life. But his record of horrible success is today approaching the 2000-year mark, and comparatively few suspect the truth!

The story began at Golgotha, known as the place of the skull—probably because a rock formation in the hillside resembled a human skull. Most often we call it Calvary, which is an English word derived from the same meaning—skull.

Jesus of Nazareth, crucified there, had just died. And I picture Satan, the rebel chief, sitting in the shadows not far away—absolutely dejected. He had lost the battle. He knew it. He knew that his doom was sealed!

You would expect him to be happy, wouldn't you? After all, it was he who was the chief instigator of the crucifixion.

Yes, he wanted Him crucified, but I'm not sure he wanted Him to die. He probably wanted to push Jesus to the limit, short of death, hoping that He would call it quits—not worth it—and return to heaven.

You see, Satan's purpose was to defeat the plan for man's salvation. All the way from Bethlehem to Golgotha the evil angel had hounded the steps of Jesus, trying to discourage Him, trying to trip Him up, trying to get Him to sin if only by a word, trying to get Him to quit.

In the first place, he had thought that God would certainly never bother with the fallen race. The cry of a lost and lonely planet would stir no lasting sympathy in the heart of the Almighty. It was incomprehensible to the rebel's selfish mind that the Son of God would be concerned enough to come down here and die in man's place so that he could live. Selfishness has trouble understanding love. And Satan seemed to think that if he just made things miserable enough, Jesus would surely turn back and abandon His plan to save men. The human race would then be left to certain destruction. And nothing delights the rebel chief more than mass destruction.

Satan knew that Jesus could easily work a miracle to deliver Himself from His enemies. He knew that Jesus, if He chose, could easily come down from the cross and let ten thousand angels sweep Him heavenward in the sight of His tormentors.

But Jesus didn't quit. He didn't come down from the cross. He stayed there to the last and let the world's sins crush out His life. And Satan wasn't stupid. He knew that his mask had been torn away. In the eyes of the universe he had now been exposed as a murderer—the murderer of his own Creator. He could expect no sympathy now, ever again, from the unfallen worlds.

Satan hated the cross. He hated it with an intensity that cannot be described. But there, in the shadow of the instrument of death that had sealed his doom, he hit upon the same idea that Ramses had used to feed his pride. He had lost the battle. But he would make it appear he had won. He would concoct his own story of what happened at Golgotha. He would repaint the cross. He would misinterpret it, distort its meaning, and promote worldwide misunderstanding by means of massive propaganda. *He would make the cross he hated a weapon against God!*

You see, Satan's rebellion from the beginning has been an attack upon God's authority, His government, and His law. In his encounter with our first parents, in Eden, it was a direct command of God that was so brazenly questioned. And in these last days, according to the book of Revelation, it will still be the authority of God that is at issue. It will still be the people who accept God's authority and keep His commands—it is these who will be the target of the rebel angel's greatest wrath. See Revelation 12:17.

Lucifer, when first he rebelled, campaigned for the repeal of God's law. But how could God repeal a law that is a transcript of His own character, a law that is the foundation of His government? How could God alter in any way a law so important, so perfect, so unchangeable, so sacred that its violation could not be overlooked even to save His own Son from Calvary?

Tell me. Isn't it strange to contend that the cross cancels out the law or in any way weakens it? Can you believe that God would let His own Son die because the law could not be changed—and then turn around and change it as soon as His Son was dead? Hardly!

Ask the apostle Paul, and he will tell you that God's law is "holy, and the commandment holy, and just, and good." Romans 7:12, KJV. Ask David, and he will tell you that "the law of the Lord is perfect, converting the soul." Psalm 19:7, KJV. Another psalm will tell you that all of God's commandments "stand fast for ever and ever." Psalm 111:8, KJV. And God Himself says, "My covenant will I not break, nor alter the thing that is gone out of my lips." Psalm 89:34, KJV. He tells us this about Himself: "I am the Lord, I change not." Malachi 3:6, KJV.

There is no way to separate the integrity of God's law from the integrity of God Himself. They stand or fall together!

Satan well knew that God's law would not, and could not, be set aside. He had just witnessed, in the death of Jesus, the mightiest argument of all for the unchangeable nature of the divine law. For if the law could have been set aside, Jesus need not have died!

In the light of all this knowledge, and much more, the once-brilliant angel conceived his bold and reprehensible scheme there at Golgotha. He would tell the world that the cross he hated, the cross that had sealed his doom, the cross that had upheld the law at the cost of the Creator's lifeblood, had in reality given him everything he wanted. He would tell the world that the purpose of Calvary had been to remove God's law, that God had decided, after all, to free men from its restrictions and give them liberty to do as they pleased!

Satan knew that the cross he hated would be honored by all Christians, that the story of God's dying in man's place would be told and retold through every generation, that men through all time would preach and pray and sing about it. But the rebel chief cared not. He would gladly join in their praise of Calvary's sacrifice—so long as it was misunderstood, so long as its meaning was distorted, so long as it could be turned to the advantage of his rebellion.

Satan would picture Sinai, with its thunder and smoke, as the work of a harsh and tyrannical God, and Calvary as the work of a loving Saviour. He would pit one against the other—as if Sinai were a mistake that had to be corrected at Calvary. He would contend that Sinai was law and Calvary was grace. And he would be delighted as he saw men making of grace an excuse to sin. He would remind men repeatedly of what the apostle Paul said about Christians being "not under the law, but under grace," hoping they would never notice Paul's very next words: "What then? Shall we sin, because we are not under the law, but under grace? God forbid." Romans 6:14, 15, KJV.

Yes, Satan would actually pirate the grace of God that enables us to keep the law, and market it as a license to sin!

The rebel chief would stop at nothing. He would foist upon the world the notion that God has actually abolished His constitution, thrown away His moral standard, and left men to follow their own inclinations.

But it is precisely that notion—that we are subject only to our own inclinations, our own feelings—it is that notion, eagerly accepted and passed on from one generation to another, that has made our streets unsafe and our homes armed fortresses. And in our rush to permissiveness we have rejected the only answer to the epidemic of crime that surrounds us!

But obedience is not popular today. It is not sophisticated enough for this permissive society. We prefer to talk about love. We have not escaped the infection of easy religion that makes of us no demands. The shocking thing is that the cross of Calvary has been so manipulated as to help create this situation!

Isn't it a tragedy that the cross which cost the lifeblood of

Jesus that stands as the ultimate in obedience to the Father's will, should be so misunderstood? Isn't it frightening that the very sacrifice which has forever established the authority and unchanging character of God's law should be represented as destroying it? How is it that millions can be so blinded? But here will come the last great deception. Here will be the issue in the last great conflict that will separate the loyal from the disloyal.

Yes, Satan will fight the cross while pretending to love it. He will gladly join in praise of what happened that dark day on Golgotha's hill. But all the while he is going for the jugular—using the cross that sealed his doom as an unsuspected weapon in his desperate and insane attempt to dethrone God!

From old England comes an account of a young boy named Bron who went to church for the first time with his governess.

The minister climbed high into the pulpit and then told a piece of terrible news. He told how an innocent Man had been nailed to a cross and left to die.

How terrible, the lad thought! How wrong! Surely the people would do something about it. But he looked about him and no one seemed concerned. They must be waiting for church to be over, he decided. Then surely they would do something to right this horrible deed.

He walked out of church trembling with emotion, waiting to see what the crowd would do. And his governess said, "Bron, don't take it to heart. Someone will think you are strange!"

Strange—to be upset, disturbed by injustice? Strange—to be stirred by so tragic a recital? Strange—to care, and want desperately to do something about it?

Shame on us for our casual, superficial commitments—left at the door of the church and forgotten! There is something to be done about what happened at Calvary. Jesus said, "If ye love me, keep my commandments!" John 14:15, KJV.

Love is more than what you say. Love is something you do!

And now in our search to distinguish truth from propaganda we turn to the record of our origins. These next few chapters will be a necessary revelation if we are to fully understand the deep significance of the final chapters of this book.

Tying Down the Sun

Three Santa Barbara homes—homes with the choicest view and valued at several hundred thousands of dollars each—tumbled unceremoniously into the Pacific Ocean. All it took was a series of rainstorms!

Theories, too—even some that masquerade as fact—have a way of eroding with time, showing dangerous cracks, and finally washing away, or toppling headlong under the bombardment of questions that cannot be answered.

But the passing of a theory is seldom mourned. It is only replaced. And it isn't long until the replacement topples too. So what can we believe? That's the question. Your theory is as good as mine—and mine as good as yours.

Wouldn't it be helpful if some final authority would just walk in and set us straight? Wouldn't it be helpful if God would arrange a spectacular thunderbolt fanfare—and then step out on a cloud and tell everybody that your ideas—or mine—are correct? Wouldn't we like that? How it would simplify matters!

Of course some ideas still around today, and sincerely believed, would never get that kind of vindication. Some of them are so precariously founded that they do little more than trigger a smile.

You have probably heard of the man who walked the streets of New York City always snapping his fingers. Someone asked him why he was doing it, and he replied, "To keep the lions away." He was reminded that there hadn't been any lions on the streets of New York for a long time. And to that he answered triumphantly, "Effective, isn't it?"

45

Did you know that the Flat Earth Society has a hundred members? A hundred people who presumably actually believe that the earth is flat!

And did you know that residents of a small Turkish village still fire shots at the sun during a solar eclipse? According to an old tradition, a dragon is trying to steal the sun, and the shots are supposed to frighten off the beast. One villager explained, "We don't actually believe it anymore, but it's nice to keep up the tradition."

Dragons die hard!

But here's the most interesting one I've come across. Listen to this. Did you know that the ancient Incas, each year at the time of the southern solstice, performed a ceremony in which they tied down the sun?

You see, the Incas worshiped the sun. It was their god. But it kept going farther and farther south, and they were afraid it would get away. So the priests would symbolically tie it down in their capital city—to what they called "the hitching-post of the sun." And sure enough, it worked! Immediately the sun would begin going north again!

And of course the ceremony didn't work at all. All it proved was that they knew the day of the southern solstice!

Is it possible that some of us are holding to some theories that aren't as well founded as we wish they were?

We seem to be fascinated with the possibility that sometime, somehow, somewhere—perhaps in a dramatic encounter deep in space—we might discover the facts, and even some of the details, of our origin. We can't stop wanting to know!

Are we here by accident? Is our planet the child of a straying sun? Is life a slow train through the ages, with the passengers knowing neither where or why or when they boarded, nor what their destination is? Have the chains of uniformity fated us to eternal boredom—with change and adventure taboo?

Or did our ride on this planet have a spectacular beginning the day God personally stood on our little earth and said, "Let Us make man in Our image"? Has our past been interrupted by the catastrophe of a global flood, and our history cut in two by the wonder and the pathos of Bethlehem? Will the wind-up of this planet's turbulent flight be equally as spectacular as its beginning?

If only God would step out on a thundercloud and flash the lightning in our eyes and convince us?

Or if only the gods of accident and chance would stop their pretending and demonstrate, once for all, that they are responsible for our presence here!

Whether it be a jet or a mountain, a baby or a sunbeam, a boulder or a rose, we seem to think there are but two possibilities. Either we made it or it just happened. Are we unwilling that there should be any creator but ourselves? Is that our problem?

This rebel planet would like to forget its God. It denies His existence and questions His dealings and quibbles about His words. It alternately buries and resurrects Him. But it seems strangely unable to put Him out of its mind!

Why all this preoccupation with God? Why all this talk about God by men who do not believe in Him? Is there a hunger within the hate?

These questioning minds are like the Russian girl who was brought up an atheist. She had just written a government examination and, like all students, was concerned about some of the answers she had given. The question that had troubled her most was this: "What is the inscription on the Sarmian Wall?" She had written, "Religion is the opiate of the people." But she wasn't sure; so she walked the seven miles to the Sarmian Wall and checked. There it was: "Religion is the opiate of the people." In her relief she forgot her atheism and exclaimed, "Thank God! I had it right!"

They are like the girl who says of her boyfriend, "Oh, we're not speaking anymore. I've lost all interest in him. We haven't spoken for three days, six hours, and twenty-three minutes!"

Not speaking anymore. But just try to get her more than ten feet from the phone!

That's this planet. Through with its God. Not speaking anymore. But forever listening for His ring!

Through with Him? Not yet. And not quite!

Did He or Didn't He?

On a number of occasions I have visited the state of Hawaii. I have stood on its beaches, fascinated by its picture-book coastline and the indescribable blue of the seas. I have tasted its exotic fruits and wondered at the incomparable beauty of its flowers.

I have also walked on lava not yet completely cooled. I stood at the rim of a crater and looked down into boiling fire only about a hundred feet below. These islands, of course, are volcanic islands born in violence. Repeatedly I saw the marks of a catastrophic past. Again and again I could only say, "Something has happened here!"

Probably nowhere else in the world is there such a blend of catastrophe and creation, of violence and calm, of chaos and exotic beauty. Hawaii, to some minds, seems a product of long, slow ages of accident and chance. After all, would a loving Creator make a planet so prone to catastrophe, a planet that for millenniums would spew out fire and smoke and rivers of molten rock—and call it good?

Yet beside these marks of violence and destruction, even wedged among them, we seem to find the remnants of a paradise once lost. It is as if the Creator, unwilling to be forgotten, had gathered some of the most exotic samples of His handiwork and placed them on exhibit here. It matters not whether the seeds of such beauty were born here or blown here or brought here—what else can they be but the work of an intelligent and loving God?

49

It is not surprising that the early Hawaiians tried to explain their strange new world. The Polynesians found in these islands phenomena that they had not experienced in the homeland from which they had come. They were not used to the thunder of great volcanoes that sent forth geysers of flaming lava.

From the southern islands they had brought a variety of gods—a god of war, a god of agriculture, a god for fishermen and sailors, and thousands of household gods. But now they needed a god of fire.

So they came to believe that Pele, a goddess from their ancient homeland of Kahiki, was responsible for volcanic activity. One story has it that in Kahiki the goddess had failed to show respect for the sacred land and had burned it; so she was expelled by her brothers. She came north to the little island of Kaula and tunneled into the earth, but found no place where her fire could be sustained. Next she traveled southeastward, always hoping to find a deep hole where her fire would take hold. On the island of Maui she dug the great crater of Haleakala. But again she had no lasting success. So at last she crossed the channel to the island of Hawaii. Here she found Kilauea, and was satisfied. So the pit of Kilauea, a nearly always active, or at least smoldering caldera, is said to be the home of the fire goddess.

The ancient Hawaiians believed that the goddess needed to be appeased when she became violent. So even today, when there is an eruption, you might see a Hawaiian throw twigs of ohelo or a red handkerchief into the caldera to ease the anger of the ancient deity.

There is another tradition that interested me especially. It concerns Haleakala, on the island of Maui, which we mentioned a moment ago, and which last erupted sometime after 1750. Haleakala means literally "house of the sun." "Tradition has it," writes Edward Joesting in the book *Eternal Hawaii*, "that Maui, the trickster demi-god of all Polynesia, was annoyed with the sun, which sped too fast across the sky. His mother, Hina, had difficulty drying the bark-cloth, or kapa, she made. The days were too short to provide sufficient warmth.

"So, Maui devised a plan. He knew that the golden shafts of light seen early in the day were the sun's legs. One by one, as they appeared through the clouds at the top of Koolau Gap, he snared them and bound them fast to an ohia tree. The sun, thus entrapped, pleaded for release, but Maui relented only after the sun promised to slow his daily march."

Again, *tying down the sun!*

Hawaii, of course, is not the only place on this planet that seems to demand an explanation of its past. All over this earth there are phenomena that we do not fully understand. Sheer escarpments, boulders tumbled in chaotic formations, sea life high in mountain ranges, water lines where they don't seem to belong, all have one message: "Something has happened here!"

No one can stand on the rim of the Grand Canyon and not wonder what it was. And there's the High Sierra range—in my own state of California. It is impossible to visit it, even the first time, without the strong, deep feeling that *something has happened here.* Something tremendous, something catastrophic, something beyond the reach of imagination. Said one visitor, "This whole country is standing on end!"

What happened—to make the whole country stand on end? What were the forces that created this bold, dramatic, wild, beautifully disordered landscape? We try to explain it. Are our explanations more credible than those of the ancient Hawaiians?

It was not so long ago that a Sequoia National Park ranger strolled into a crowd of about three hundred who had made the climb from the Owens Valley to the granite summit of Mount Whitney. One of the hikers, simply awed by the sight of the two-mile plunge down to the valley floor, asked the ranger how the Sierra came to be shaped as it is.

The ranger had had a smattering of geology, and he replied, "Well, this summit plateau is part of the old landscape that was lying here as kind of a rolling lowland millions of years ago. Then the whole Sierra was bowed up like an arch." More people turned to listen, and he went on, "Then the keystone collapsed to form this great escarpment going down into the Owens Valley, with the White Mountains over there to the east making the other half of the broken arch. And later, through erosion and glaciation we got the final shaping of the land—the meadows and canyons and peaks and bowls—as you see them all around you today."

The ranger paused to let all that information soak in, and one of the hikers spoke up and said, "I don't believe anything you say. The Bible says the Lord made the world in six days, so nothing you say is true!"

Now the outspoken hiker might more logically have suggested that the convulsions of the earth at the time of Noah's Flood might be a better explanation. For the question under discussion was not how the Sierra *came to be*, but *how it came to be shaped as it is*.

But the ranger didn't challenge the hiker's faulty logic—if in fact he was even aware of it. The real issue was the reliability of the Bible record. And evidently he felt no inclination to challenge that, at least not at the moment. Instead he replied thoughtfully, "Well, yes, it does. It says that." And he wandered off by himself to think about it. Months later he hadn't thought of a more suitable reply. "What could I tell the guy?" he shrugged. "Besides, maybe he was right!"

And Ezra Bowen, who tells the story in his book *The High Sierra*, comments, "Maybe he was." He says that "today the most sophisticated earth scientists, not to mention the fundamentalists, are still groping among the particulars of the Sierra's creation."

Yes, the hiker might have been more tactful. But it's true that an ancient, neglected Book, the Book we call the Bible, tells us all we really need to know about our past. And it may be that even the Sequoia ranger realized that the account we find in that ancient Book is far less complicated, far more reasonable, far easier to believe than the popular but changing theories of the geologists who probe among the rocks for the answers.

How simply the Bible tells it:

"In the beginning God created the heaven and the earth." Genesis 1:1.

"By the word of the Lord the heavens were made, and by the breath of His mouth all their host. . . . For He spoke, and it was done; He commanded, and it stood fast." Psalm 33:6-9, NASB.

"For in six days the Lord made heaven and earth." Exodus 20:11.

"And God saw every thing that he had made, and, behold, it was very good." Genesis 1:31.

"And the waters prevailed exceedingly upon the earth; and all the high hills, that were under the whole heaven, were covered. Fifteen cubits upward did the waters prevail; and the mountains were covered." Genesis 7:19, 20.

There it is. Our past in clear, simple outline. In words that a child can understand. Our God created this earth in six days. It was very good. But fifteen hundred years later, because men had become so corrupt, God found it necessary to destroy all but eight persons. And He did it by means of a global Flood.

Tell me. Do we have to study the rocks on the moon, do we have to probe deep into outer space, to discover how our planet came to be—and why it appears as it does today? Do we have to spend millions of dollars searching for the answers? Why haven't we listened to the one Book that claims to be the word of the Creator Himself? Why haven't we given it a second thought? Why haven't we checked it out? Why have we written it off as myth or legend? Is the explanation too simple for our sophisticated minds?

"In the beginning God created the heaven and the earth."

Did He or didn't He? That's the question. That's what we have to decide. And our lives will be profoundly affected by our decision!

But keep in mind the implications of a negative answer. For if we say that God didn't do what He says He did, then it means that God didn't tell the truth. It means that the Bible is wrong. It means that the Bible is a book of falsehoods!

And it means, too, that we have no Saviour and no hope. For if you throw out Genesis, you must throw out the cross of Calvary too. The Bible says that *"all scripture* is given by inspiration of God." 2 Timothy 3:16, emphasis supplied.

So it's all or nothing. If Genesis goes, our hope goes too. But who wants to throw away his hope, and his future, in an hour like this?

We read, "And God said, Let there be light: and there was light." Genesis 1:3.

Did God turn on the light? Or didn't He? Did God turn on the light? Or did Darwin?

And then I ask another question. If God did create this world, as He says He did, did He do a good job? Or did He bungle it?

Repeatedly, in the first chapter of Genesis, we read, "And God saw that it was good." Was it? Or wasn't it? Would God have called it good if the survival of His creation was to be dependent on the whims of long ages of accident and chance? And would God have called it good if it appeared as it does today—with the marks of catastrophe everywhere? Or has something catastrophic, something God never intended, happened *between then and now* to a creation that, when God finished it, was very, very good?

Nowhere is there a more beautiful valley than Yosemite. It seems not to belong in this world. No one who has ever seen its white granite walls gleaming in the moonlight will ever forget the sight. Those walls of monolithic rock rise on either side from 3000 to 4800 feet above the valley floor—El Capitan, Half Dome, Sentinel Rock, Glacier Point!

But did God create it as it is now—in all the disorder and desolation and disarray? No. As you see the High Sierra today, you can only conclude that, beautiful and grand as it is, whatever has happened here is something that was never meant to be!

John Muir thought glaciers were responsible. But the cantankerous Josiah Whitney, after whom Mount Whitney was named, said, "No glaciers." He was very sure of himself. He was especially sure that Yosemite Valley had been created by a monstrous collapse of the earth floor.

Was it? The great earthquake of March, 1872, gave us some indication of the awesome force it would take to create Yosemite Valley. For several hours severe tremors rumbled through the high country. The Owens Valley was split in a way that brought sheer terror to all who lived in it. Of course, not many people were living anywhere near. That's the only reason there was not a tremendous loss of life.

A forty-acre field sank seven feet. A small lake disappeared. The Owens River ran upstream for a time until its bed was dry. In the darkness, according to one account, "people watched cascades of rock roaring down the mountains in monstrous avalanches, throwing out such brilliant trails of sparks that they were assumed to be flows of lava."

Yosemite was a hundred and twenty miles from the epicenter, but still well within the scope of its convulsions. There was a tremendous roar as the Eagle Rock on the south wall gave way. Thousands of great boulders poured to the valley floor in a sort of free curve—friction giving it the appearance of an arc of glowing fire!

The roar of scraping rock was indescribable. Trying to give some idea of the volume of the awful sound, John Muir, who experienced it, said, "It seems to me that if all the thunder of all the storms I have ever heard were condensed into one roar it would not equal this rock roar!"

This Owens Valley earthquake of 1872 was one of the great earthquakes of all history. But it brought little change to the face of the Sierra. Other than the rockslides, the most noticeable scar on the whole Sierra—after this giant earthquake—was "one wistful little breast work threading across three miles of the Owens Valley floor and rising perhaps 23 feet at the highest point."

Think of it! All this sound and fury. And it left a mark three miles long and at most twenty-three feet high. The Sierra scarp looming over Lone Pine is almost five hundred times that high. What would it have taken to shape the Sierra as we see it today? How many earthquakes would it take to carve out Yosemite—Half Dome, El Capitan, and all? Evidently earthquakes as presently conceived could never have produced these features.

There must be some better answers than those the geologists have been repeating—many of the geologists, that is. Some are beginning to wonder. Says Ezra Bowen, "California's earth scientists recently fell to doubting whether there had ever been a Sierra arch at all, with keystones that collapsed to form the eastern valley; or whether the whole range had not been built by some other force not yet fathomed."

What do you think of that? "Some other force not yet fathomed." But God tells us what that other force was. The book of Genesis says, "More and more the waters increased over the earth until they covered all the high mountains everywhere under heaven. The waters increased and the mountains were covered to a depth of fifteen cubits." Genesis 7:19, 20, NEB.

Water enough to cover all the high mountains everywhere. That's a lot of water! And some of you know by experience that water can be very, very violent!

This wasn't a quiet little rainstorm. The water didn't just quietly rise until it covered the mountains. More than water was involved. This was global catastrophe!

The trouble is that there is nothing in our experience that can qualify us to understand the Flood. The entire planet was involved. The earth was torn and twisted and convulsed in a way that our imagination simply cannot reach. Start with rain. Add cloudbursts. Add water gushing forth from the earth. Add tidal waves. Add fire. Add wind. Add volcanoes. Add twisting and turning. Add mountains rising and falling. Add the most violent convulsions, the wildest upheavals. Add everything you can think of. And we still cannot begin to appreciate what happened in Noah's day. Not a catastrophe of a moment. Rather, it must have been centuries before the earth quieted down!

God says this planet, because of rebellion against its God, has suffered a global catastrophe. Has it? Or hasn't it? Can we believe God? Or can't we?

God looked at His creation when He had finished it and said it was good, very good. Was it?

The truth is that even with all the scars of global catastrophe, along with all the marks that our own grubby fingers have left on the beauty spots of this planet—Hawaii, the High Sierra, and all the rest—God's creation still hasn't lost its grandeur. Even when torn and twisted and heaved and tossed and stood on end, it still bears the signature of a loving Creator. Its beauty still holds us spellbound!

Did God create this planet as He said He did? In six literal days? Was there a global Flood? It makes a difference how we answer!

There are those who would like to have it both ways. They would like to believe in God—and evolution too. They would like to believe that this planet was here, with the long, slow processes of evolution doing their work, millions or billions of years before God came personally on the scene as described in the book of Genesis. But have they really thought through the implications of such a compromise?

If living creatures were dying and fossils being laid down in the rocks long before Adam and Eve, then death was here before sin. In that case God has misrepresented the facts in telling us that death is the result of sin. In that case man doesn't need a Saviour after all, and the gospel of Christ is meaningless. Do we really want to go that far? Is it possible, simultaneously, to hold onto concepts of our beginnings that are headed in opposite directions? Or must we make a choice?

Why is it that some of us are so *willing* to believe that sub-human ancestors to man lived on this planet in the distant past when only meager and highly questionable evidence can be contrived? Yet there is a widespread *reluctance* to believe the record of a global catastrophe in the days of Noah, even though we read it in a divinely inspired Book—and even though *its marks can still be seen,* written indelibly into the surface of our planet.

It makes a difference, I say, what we believe about the past. For if catastrophe and heartache and suffering and death were here before sin, they can hardly be blamed to sin—and God has misled us.

It makes a difference what we believe. For if we believe that we are the offspring of chance, nothing more than educated animals, then moral degeneracy is inevitable. Can animals, no matter how sophisticated, be expected to answer to any moral code?

It makes a difference what we believe. For what we believe about creation determines what we believe about the character of God. Do we think of God as a capricious and impersonal deity who made a world and set it running and then went off and left it, caring nothing for the creatures He had made? Or do we see in the book of Genesis a loving Creator who, as soon as man sinned, provided a Saviour? It makes a difference!

"For in six days the Lord made heaven and earth." Did He? "And God saw that it was good." Was it?

Saith the ancient Job, "Go and ask the cattle, ask the birds of the air to inform you, or tell the creatures that crawl to teach you, and the fishes of the sea to give you instruction. Who cannot learn from all these that the Lord's own hand has done this?" Job 12:7-9, NEB.

An unbeliever, so the story goes, was doing a little boasting. He said to a Christian, "We're going to destroy all your churches and burn all your Bibles. We won't leave you a thing to remind you of your God."

The Christian said nothing. He only looked up toward the sky and smiled. The boaster was annoyed. "Why are you smiling?" "I'm just wondering," said the Christian, "how you're going to get the stars down!"

Yes, how can you get the stars down? Or erase the memory of the rocks? Or quiet the dance of the honeybee? Or explain the construction of the birds?

Born to Fly

The construction of a fighter plane is incredibly precise. The type of wing. The sweep of the wing. The structure of the tail. The engine housing. And of course the weight. All must be right—if it is to fly.

But did you know that the tiny sparrow in your back yard has been constructed even more precisely—for flight?

A sparrow isn't worth much, by some standards. In the days of Christ you could buy two of them for a penny. And yet Jesus said that not one of them falls to the ground without His Father's notice.

And we say, "That's love. That's care. You'd expect a loving God to notice even an insignificant sparrow."

But did you know that a sparrow has already had considerable attention—before it first takes to the sky? In fact, it seems evident that God used as much care in constructing the sparrow as He did in creating the world.

You see, sparrows were never meant to fall to the ground. They were designed for flight!

And so were nearly all birds. (Penguins, a notable exception, are superbly designed for "flying" in water.)

According to an ancient Greek myth, an Athenian man named Daedalus and his son Icarus both fell out of favor with the king of Crete. They were exiled on a small island in the Mediterranean Sea. Naturally they sought some way to escape.

Daedalus, the story says, carefully studied the design of the wings of the sea birds. Then he made two pairs of wings cut of wax and feathers. These wings enabled them to escape. But it all ended in disaster when Icarus, excited with his new ability to fly, flew too near the sun. The poet says,

> With melting wax and loosened strings,
> Sank hapless Icarus on unfaithful wings.

It was three thousand years later that man learned to fly. But it wasn't by attaching wings to his body. A man simply isn't designed to fly. And it would take more than wings to change that situation.

For one thing, the breast muscles that operate a man's shoulders and arms weigh less than one percent of his total body weight. But those muscles in some birds may make up 30 percent of the total body weight.

The bones of a bird, on the other hand, are very light. And they are hollow. For instance, although the man-o'-war bird has a wing span of about seven feet, its bones weigh only four or five ounces. Think of it! Its plumage actually weighs more than its skeleton. And feathers are light, you know.

Yet in spite of the lightness of a bird's bones, they are unusually flexible and strong. And of course these are features that are essential to cope with the stresses and strains of flight.

You realize, of course, that tremendous energy is demanded for flight. But here again, birds are well equipped. They have the highest body temperatures of any animal. This high body temperature, along with an efficient digestive system and rapid circulation, means that birds can utilize an unusually high percentage of the food they eat.

Someone has calculated that the golden plover is so efficient it can migrate thousands of miles across the ocean from Labrador to the central part of South America by losing only about two ounces of its body weight. If a small airplane could do as well, it would get about 160 miles to a gallon of gasoline instead of twenty miles to the gallon as it now does!

There must, of course, be rapid delivery of energy to the breast muscles. But it seems that nothing is overlooked. Birds have a higher blood pressure than men, and blood-sugar concentrations are about twice that of mammals. Weak-flying birds, such as domestic chickens, have a relatively poor blood supply to the breast muscles. That's why the flesh is pale in color. But strong fliers have good circulation in these muscles, and the muscle is dark red in color.

And then, of course, for flight there must be keen eyesight. But that's all cared for. In some hawks and other birds of prey, vision is eight to ten times more efficient than in humans. This doesn't mean that hawks have telescopic vision. But it does mean that the eye is constructed for greater resolving power. The most sensitive part of a hawk's eye contains up to a million and a half visual cells—while a man's eye has only 200,000. You can see why a hawk is able to distinguish detail.

A bird's feathers are amazingly structured for protection against heat and cold, for fanning the air, and for streamlining the body. And every slight change in position of a feather during flight is designed to absorb energy from the air and use it effectively. It is estimated that, for their weight, feathers are stronger than any man-made material. Below the contour feathers of the body, many birds are provided with an undercoat of very soft feathers that serve as insulation.

If you inspect the construction of a single wing feather under a microscope, you will see a truly marvelous design. That feather is extremely complex in both structure and function. We are told that a single pigeon primary wing feather has more than a million parts. There are vanes and barbs and barbules and flanges and tiny hooks. And all work together to form a zipper. When it becomes unzipped, it can be zipped up again by preening.

Next time you find a feather somewhere, remember that it is amazingly designed to give strength and flexibility in flight.

But that isn't all. As a bird flies, every slight change in air flow is automatically compensated. The flight feathers of the wing tip act like the propeller of an airplane. They change pitch to cope with the changing stresses that the air exerts upon them. The base part of the wing acts like the wing of a plane. And the secondary and tertiary wing feathers function as flaps.

But now listen. Embedded in the skin near the quill of each flight feather are nerve endings that actually convert the feathers into sensory receptors. They record the precise position of every feather. And then, by way of the spinal cord, they bring about continuous adjustment in the more than 12,000 tiny muscles that are attached to the base of the feathers!

But wait. That still isn't all. The precise body position of the bird is recorded by the semicircular canals of the inner ear. And the inner ear reports the changing conditions to the cerebellum of the bird's brain. What do you think of that?

When you watch a bird in flight, it's very difficult to tell just what is going on. The form of the wing is constantly changing. And of course we can't see the internal muscular movements.

In general, the larger the bird, the slower it flaps its wings. A hummingbird vibrates its wings about fifty times per second, and a heron only about two times. Take-off and landing naturally demand the greatest energy and coordination.

Gliding flight is much like a toboggan sliding downhill—except that the bird is sliding on air instead of on snow. Here's how it works. If a bird is gliding down an airslope losing altitude at the rate of ten feet per second, but the region of air which contains the airslope is rising ten feet per second at the same time, the bird will glide along in a level flight. And of course if the air is rising faster than the bird is gliding downhill, the bird will gain altitude without any effort.

If the wind speed equals the forward and downward speed of a gliding bird, the bird will appear to stand still. It is as if a man were walking down an up escalator at the same speed it moves up. His progress in space is zero.

You may have noticed soaring birds with their wing tips spread like fingers on a hand. This is called slotting. It serves to prevent turbulence behind the wings when the wings are tilted downward. It is necessary when a bird is coming in for a landing.

Then there are the helicopter actions of some birds—vertical, reverse, and hovering flights. These are extremely complicated patterns of coordination that we don't fully understand. We do know that these acrobats of the air use not only a powered downstroke but also a powered upstroke.

I don't know about you, but I'm absolutely amazed! Birds—whether sparrows or hummingbirds, hawks, or eagles—are born to fly. They are fantastically *equipped* to fly. They are intricately *made* to fly!

And right here I would like to thank my friend, the ornithologist Dr. Asa Thoresen, for all this fascinating information about birds!

Is it any wonder that God challenged ancient Job with the question, "Is it by your understanding that the hawk soars, stretching his wings toward the south? Is it at your command that the eagle mounts up, and makes his nest on high? On the cliff he dwells and lodges, upon the rocky crag, an inaccessible place. From there he spies out food; his eyes see it from afar. . . . and where the slain are, there is he." Job 39:26-30, NASB.

Tell me. Did all this come about by chance? Did birds just develop all these capabilities over long ages? Did their fantastic equipment for flight come about little by little?

Think it through. Suppose a bird had the right kind of wings, but his breast muscles were weak. Would he be able to fly? What if he had no way of getting energy to these muscles quickly? Could he fly? What if the bird had poor eyesight? What then?

What if a bird's feathers were simply constructed—like scales on a fish or a reptile, for instance? What if these feathers were not so intricately made that the form of the wings could constantly change? And what if these changes were not recorded in the inner ear and sent on to the brain for perfect coordination? If even one piece of the bird's equipment were missing, or not fully developed, could he fly?

In other words, if a bird had some of the necessary flight equipment, but not all of it, could he function some way in the meantime while he waited for the missing equipment to develop? No. He needs it all at once. He has to be *born* that way. He has to be *made* that way. And that, friend, isn't evolution. It's creation! It's "in the beginning God!"

It was Job, you recall, who suggested, "Ask the birds of the air to inform you." Job 12:7, NEB.

Ask the birds. Watch them in flight. Study the way they are made. The message is too clear to be missed. There *is* a God. There *is* a Creator. There *is* meaning to life. The birds didn't just happen. They aren't the product of blind, mindless, meaningless, haphazard chance. And neither are we!

But first—a seconding speech from the honeybee!

Who Told the Honeybee?

Computers and rockets and dictionaries and planes are the product of genius and hard work. But the men who design them are the product of accident and chance. So we are told.

But did you know that the common honeybee, without even trying, can upset the conclusions of brilliant minds?

Just how much are you willing to attribute to the unlikely magic of the ages? If evolution happened, *how* did it happen? Would it be unreasonable to ask some specific questions—in one small area?

Come with me as we watch the fascinating activities of the common honeybee. I promise there will be some surprises—and a rather formidable dilemma for those who credit all creation to the supposed power of time to do in the past what it cannot do now!

Have you ever noticed that bees are incredible architects? The hive is a masterpiece of engineering, with rows and rows of six-sided rooms with walls of wax.

The marble palace that we call the comb is built by young bees under seventeen days old. Yet each little room is the same size, six-sided, with each of three pairs of walls facing the other. The walls of the rooms are only 1/350th of an inch thick, yet so strong that one pound of comb will support at least twenty-five pounds of honey.

How do these young bees know that the hexagon has the smallest circumference, therefore requiring the smallest amount of building material? How do they know that hexagon

65

cells are the best and most economical plan? Who told them? Yet they do it all without blueprints or drawing boards or protractors. And every cell is perfect—just the size to fit a bee!

How do they do it? They hang themselves up like a festoon from the roof of the hive. Or it may be in the hollow of a tree. One bee hooks onto the roof, and another bee hooks onto his dangling legs, and so on. These chains of bees grow longer and longer, and as they sway back and forth, they hook onto bees on the right and left until they form a living curtain.

They hang themselves up like this to produce wax. You see, there are four wax pockets on each side of the bee's abdomen. And after about twenty-four hours of hanging, wax begins to appear from these pockets. When a bee feels its wax is ready, it climbs up over the other bees, takes the wax out of its pockets, chews it, and pats it onto the comb.

At first they just pile on wax. Then they form rough cups, climb into them, and push. And apparently all this pushing sets up vibrations which enable the bees to judge the elasticity and thickness of the walls. The result—the perfect shape and the incredibly thin walls. And that's the way the comb is built.

The bees perform their tasks in perfect cooperation, as if their assignments were posted on a bulletin board!

It must be a marvel of organization, you say. Yes. But who directs it?

It is true that no honeybee lives to itself. They all live for the hive. There may be forty to seventy-five thousand bees in a hive, or more, all working in perfect harmony, as a unit.

But who is the leader? Is it the queen? You might say she exerts leadership at the time of swarming. But even then the worker bees play the key role in locating a new nest site. The queen, of course, is an egg-laying machine. In a single day she can lay two thousand eggs. And evidently she does produce chemical signals that in some way enable the colony to function smoothly. For we are told that it takes less than a hundred worker bees to build a comb if the queen is present, but thousands of them if there is no queen. But is she the leader of the hive? Certainly not.

And the drones are not the leaders. These male bees are com-

pletely indolent. They spend their lifetime waiting—just waiting for a chance to chase after a queen on her mating flight.

The worker bees are unquestionably the real marvels of the
hive. But they have no leader. Yet somehow they get all the
right things done!

Bees need two things—pollen and nectar. Both are found in
flowers. And as they fly off to the fields of flowers, they go mar-
velously equipped.

In the first place, a honeybee is a fantastically engineered
flying machine. Man-made freight planes can carry a payload
of about 25 percent of their weight. But bees can carry almost
100 percent of their weight.

The bee needs no propeller or jet. Its short, wide wings both
lift and drive it. It can move straight up or down, or it can hover
in midair. Its stubby wings fold in a split second when it dives
into a flower. Or it can use its wings as a fan to cool the beehive.

The bee has three places for storing cargo. One is a tank inside its body in which it stores nectar. Then, on its hind legs, it
has two storage baskets for carrying pollen. Imagine a freight
plane with its load dangling underneath!

Are these pollen baskets something that evolved because of a
need? Well, man first wrote about the bee in the year 3000 B.C.
It had the pollen baskets then. And it hasn't changed since!

A bee can suck up a load of nectar in a minute. It takes three
minutes for it to build up two bulging loads of pollen in the
baskets on its hind legs.

How does it do it? Well, the bee dives into a flower, its body
picking up pollen by brushing past the pollen boxes. It splashes
about in the flower, and the yellow powder clings to the hairs
on its body.

But now it isn't so simple. How does it get the pollen into the
baskets? And how does it keep the pollen from blowing away in
flight? The load must be moistened, pressed together, tamped
down, and evenly balanced on each leg. But believe it or not,
the bee does it—and all the while hovering in midair or hanging by one claw!

And now the little honeybee, acting as a scout, has discovered a field of flowers and is ready to return to the hive with a

sample of the nectar and the pollen. How will it find its way back? Keep in mind that it may be several miles away, and that its search may have led it in several directions before it made its discovery. Yet now it will fly straight back to the hive!

Who told it how to do it? What sort of navigational equipment does it possess? And once back in the hive, how will it communicate to its thousands of fellow bees the location of the treasure it has found?

It is true that bees are able to distinguish odors with great skill. If a bee returns to the hive with nectar from flowers nearby, the other bees will leave the hive and fly directly to the source. And they also act as if they have an internal clock. If they discover that food is available at a particular time of day, they return for more at the same hour the next day.

But what if the flowers are several miles distant? Surely there must be some limitation to the tiny creatures' sense of smell. What then? How can the little bee get across to its fellow bees the location of the treasure it has found?

Well, you haven't heard anything yet. Let me tell you about the "waggle dance!"

Sometimes a bee returning with nectar and pollen goes through a peculiar performance that many scientists believe is its way of communicating the location of the source of nectar. It gives samples of the nectar to the other bees and gets them all excited. Then, as they watch, it does a fancy dance before them—called the waggle dance because of the way it waggles its abdomen. It goes through a figure eight across the face of the comb. And the astonishing thing is that the angle of the dance on the *vertical* comb represents the *horizontal* direction of the food source with respect to the direction of the sun.

And not only that. The number of dances per minute indicates the distance to the field. But surprisingly, the number is in reverse ratio to the distance. That is, the farther away the field, the smaller the number. In other words, if the bee goes through ten rounds in fifteen seconds, the field of flowers is three hundred feet away. But if the bee moves in slow motion, say two rounds in fifteen seconds, the flowers are almost four miles away. And listen to this. A little calculation will show that this relationship to distance is not one of simple arithmetic, but is logarithmic! What do you think of that?

What kind of brain does the little honeybee have? Who taught it to do all this? How did this tiny creature learn to relate sun angles and distances to dance-step routines? And if one bee came up with such a mind-boggling idea all by itself, how did it teach the routine to other bees? And how is it that millions of bees understand the language?

Now I am aware that some scientists are not convinced that bees do understand the language. They are not convinced that this strange dance really does communicate to other bees the location of a field of flowers. I am aware of the controversy over this matter.

But if by any chance you are inclined to doubt, then consider this. A bee, by means of this dance, can communicate the location to human beings. Men can understand it. Men can watch the dance and find the field of flowers. Is that any less striking? Is it any less a miracle to communicate that information to human beings, in logarithmic terms, than to get it across to other bees? I think not!

I say again, What kind of brain does the little honeybee have? Is it an accident?

One writer suggests that if you wished to duplicate the internal circuitry of the honeybee, if you wished to match its navigational and guidance system, this is what you would need to start with: "Internal clock. Polarized-light sensor. Sun-angle-azimuth computer. Instrument for measuring true vertical. Dead-reckoning equipment. Wind-speed and direction indicator. Trigonometric calculator and tables. Air- and ground-speed indicators."

It sounds a little extravagant. But is it really—after what we have already seen of the honeybee's accomplishments?

And I wonder if you realize just how necessary the honeybee is—even to life itself. Bees, of course, could not exist without plants and flowers, with their pollen and their nectar. But it works both ways. Many kinds of plants and flowers could not exist without the bees to pollinate them. In fact, many of the most beautiful or most fruitful plants would disappear. And what a loss that would be!

Now tell me. Let's reason again. Did the honeybee, with all its fantastic equipment for its job, just happen? Through long ages? A little bit at a time?

What if the bee started out with no pollen baskets on its hind legs? What if it had the pollen baskets, but not the knee joints to press the pollen into the baskets, or the sense to know how to do it? What if it had no hairs on its body to collect the pollen—or the hairs but no way to comb off the pollen? What if it hadn't developed a nectar tank—yet? What if it had no wax-making equipment—or didn't know it was supposed to hang up in a festoon for twenty-four hours to make the wax come out? What if the wax would not withstand the high temperatures of the hive, as few waxes could? What if the bees didn't know how to make royal jelly to feed the queen—and the queen died? What if a bee couldn't find its way back to the hive—or back to a field of flowers?

The questions fairly tumble out. They are endless. I think you can see that any one piece of the bee's physical equipment might be useless without the others. To be of use, the bee's equipment and know-how would have to have developed simultaneously—not little by little!

Or—if evolution happened—consider this. That very first bee, away back there, sitting on the limb of a tree. What kind of bee was it? Was it a queen? But a queen could not reproduce without a drone with which to mate.

Was it a drone? Drones can't reproduce themselves without a queen.

A worker bee, then? Hardly. For worker bees are creatures that can't possibly reproduce themselves.

It is difficult to escape the conclusion that the whole colony would have to evolve at once, simultaneously—with every individual bee's physical equipment and know-how fully developed, ready for business!

And of course, with the honeybee as with the birds, that isn't evolution at all. That is creation!

Isn't it easier to believe the simple, uncomplicated,

straightforward statement that you find on the first page of your Bible? "In the beginning God created the heaven and the earth."

December 24, 1968, was a memorable Christmas Eve. For the first time in history men were orbiting the moon. Isn't it significant that Frank Borman, James Lovell, and William Anders, on that historic night, riding deeper in space than men had ever been, looking back on a half-full earth hanging in a limitless night—isn't it significant that they felt it appropriate to read, as their message to us, the first chapter of Genesis?

And the staff of the New York *Times* said of that broadcast from lunar orbit, "Somehow it was exactly right!"

It was some months later that I learned of a rather unusual incident that had taken place that night. Naturally a great many representatives of the press were on hand at the Space Center in Houston, some of them from foreign nations. Among them were two reporters from a country that I shall not name— a country without a Christian background.

They were very much interested in space flight, and they had been deeply impressed as the astronauts read from the first chapter of Genesis. Somehow they sensed that something important was going on.

They waited for the shift to change. Then, as a NASA official stepped out into the corridor, they approached him and asked politely if it would be possible to obtain a copy of the script from which the astronauts had read.

The NASA official replied with a straight face, "Why, yes. When you go back to your hotel room, just open the drawer of your desk or your nightstand. You will find a book bound in black. And the script from which the astronauts read is on the very first page."

And they said, "Oh, thank you so much! It was so thoughtful of NASA to provide the script in our hotel room!"

We smile. But listen. In the beginning—away back there— something happened. Something was going on. Something important. An earth was being formed. Man appeared on the scene.

To millions that day has always been a mystery. But it need

not be. God has thoughtfully provided the script. And it says, "In the beginning God created the heaven and the earth."

Yes, what could have been more right, more appropriate, more fitting on that memorable Christmas Eve, and in a day like this, than to recognize that this beautiful blue sphere on which we live rides securely in space not by accident, but because God placed it there?

God placed it there because He has a plan for it—and for every man and woman on it. For you and for me. Is there any better news?

Mistakes Are Easy

I wonder if you realize how easy it is to make mistakes when we set out to put together the answers on our own.

Paul A. Weiss, writing in *The Rockefeller Institute Review*, has come up with a rather hilarious piece of imagination about some Martians visiting our earth and trying to discover if life exists here.

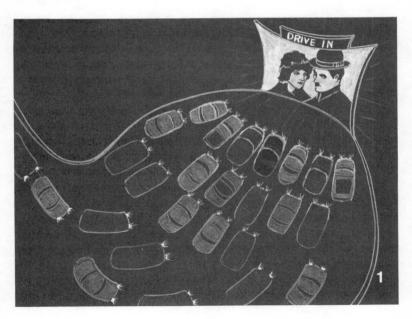

The Martians arrive at night and almost immediately find that this planet indeed is inhabited. The Earthians are wedge-shaped and move in file and unison—evidently attracted to a light source. They arrange themselves in front of this light source. (1) And then, after a few hours, the light goes out and the Earthians go back in a reverse direction.

By daylight the Martians continue their watch. They see that evidently there are parasites which live inside the Earthians. They must be parasites, because they seem unable to live long outside their host, but keep returning. (2)

The watchers see some very large Earthians (3), which must be very old. And these older Earthians have many more parasites, which proves that the parasites must multiply inside their host.

Detached from their host, these "miruses," as they call them, move very slowly and sluggishly compared to the Earthians, so the Martians decide to ignore them and concentrate on the Earthians themselves.

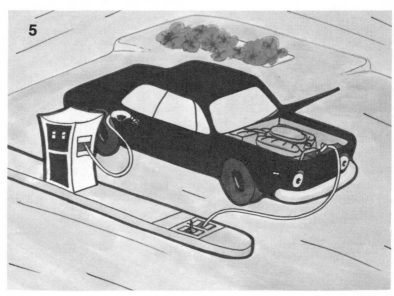

What confounds the Martians is that while most of the Earth people make contact with the ground at four points, some make contact only at two. (4) They must be degenerate forms.

They see that the Earthians do metabolize—that is, they take in substances from the environment and extract energy from them. Intake, they see, is mostly through two holes—one in front and one in back. (5) The one in front seems more important. Evidently that's where the brain is located.

One daring Martian, without being noticed, manages to reverse the two feeder tubes. The Earthian becomes completely paralyzed. And the little "miruses" become very agitated. (6) This phenomenon the Martians can't understand.

The very oldest Earthians seem to have a habit of gulping solid matter with special organs. (7)

On occasion they notice signs of grooming by the Earthians, always in front. And all members of the population start and stop the grooming process at once—as if on signal. (8)

Once in a while they see two Earthians fiercely attracted to

7

each other. They embrace in a crushing hug, and lose their shape. (9) Evidently this is a mating collision in which they give up their individual existence for some higher union.

Well, enough of that. But do you see how very easy it is to reach wrong conclusions?

And it's just as easy to make mistakes when we look back at our own beginnings. After all, we weren't there when this world was set spinning. We weren't there when life first appeared on this earth. So we can't prove that it happened this way or that. We'll have to accept somebody else's theory, or formulate one of our own. Or we must take the word of the One who says He was there and created it all. Those are the alternatives.

It's so easy to make mistakes when we start speculating about the past. We could be unquestionably sincere—and yet be as wrong as the imaginary Martians who thought cars were humans!

For instance, it's easy to assume that things have always been exactly as they are now—that things have always moved along at the same speed—that the status quo has always been the status quo.

It's easy to assume that there has never been any global catastrophe that would throw our calculations into utter confusion.

It's easy to assume that all the clocks were set at zero when time began.

It's easy to assume that the fossils were laid in their resting-places as gently as we carry the caskets of our dead.

It's easy to assume that man started out at the bottom of the ladder—physically, intellectually, socially. So we put primitive man and his primitive tools on the bottom rung and work up from there.

Millions of sincere and very intelligent people would be absolutely shocked at the suggestion that they might have the ladder bottom side up!

And yet—if we can believe the book of Genesis—man started out at the top of the ladder. He didn't start out primitive. He started out with a keener mind than any man has today. He hasn't been climbing from the bottom. He's been falling from the top!

And if he fell from the top, then what we see in those very old specimens of humanity that we've dug up and pieced together is not primitiveness but degeneracy. Not marks of a low beginning, but marks of a very great fall!

And if the book of Genesis is telling the truth—if there really was a global Flood in the days of Noah—should it surprise us that we dig up some very primitive tools from the days that followed that Flood?

Suppose, if you will, that you personally had ridden out the great storm in Noah's boat. Let's say that you were a skilled mechanic and had the most advanced tools—power-driven. But you had to leave it all behind and save your life. Then you step out onto a desolate, ravaged, watersoaked landscape to start life over again. No power. No electricity. No tools. Nothing. Wouldn't you have to make do with some hastily contrived tools that would look pretty primitive to anybody who might dig them up a few thousand years later?

And if there really was a global Flood, a global storm involving not only water but wind and fire and earthquake and volcanoes, with the earth torn and twisted and shaking and maybe not quieting down for centuries—then we can hardly assume that the status quo has always been maintained. Can we?

About those clocks. When you get a new clock and wind it up and set it going, do you always set it at twelve o'clock? Wouldn't you be just as likely to set it at five or nine or eleven?

If God made the earth in six days, as the book of Genesis says He did, then on Friday afternoon He looked out on a mature, grown-up creation, didn't He? Not redwood trees just sprouting in six-inch pots. But redwood trees that looked as if they were a thousand years old. Deer and bear and elephants already grown. Rocks that looked as if they had stood there from eternity. And if you had seen Adam, a few hours old, you would have said he was at least in his twenties!

So why should God set the clocks at zero? And if He didn't, then how can we look at those rocks today and get a true reading of their age?

You say God would be deceiving us if He set the clocks anywhere but zero? No. Hardly. How could it be deception when He has told us what He has done? It may look as if long ages were involved in the creation. But He tells us it was only six days—six literal days. So where is the deception?

And the fossils. I know. There are places where you find them right where you expect to find them—just like the table in the geology book. And it looks very convincing. But is it possible that they could be read another way? Is it possible that they were laid down not age after age but all in a single year—by the waters of a global Flood? Is it possible that the order of the fossils is not the record of ascending evolution at all—but simply the way the Flood waters sorted them out and laid them down?

Friend, I believe that a Man who was born in Bethlehem and was brought up in Nazareth is the answer to both our origin and our destiny. Our origin—because He made us. Our destiny—because He died for us!

You see, when Jesus walked the dusty roads of Palestine, it was not His first contact with this planet. He had been here before. He once said, "Before Abraham was born, I am." John 8:58, NIV.

Christ existed before Abraham was born? Evidently. In one of His prayers He said, "And now, Father, glorify me in your presence with the glory I had with you before the world began." John 17:5, NIV.

So He was with the Father before the world began. The prophet Micah said, in predicting the birth of Jesus, "But as for you, Bethlehem Ephrathah . . . from you One will go forth for Me to be ruler in Israel. His goings forth are from long ago, from the days of eternity." Micah 5:2, NASB.

The One who was born in Bethlehem was One who had existed from eternity. The apostle John calls Him the Word. He says, "In the beginning was the Word, and the Word was with God, and the Word was God. He was with God in the beginning." John 1:1, 2, NIV.

He was not only *with* God from the beginning, from eternity. He *was* God.

But are we sure John is speaking of Jesus? Yes, we are, because he says, "The Word became flesh and lived for a while among us. We have seen his glory, the glory of the one and only Son, who came from the Father, full of grace and truth." John 1:14, NIV.

Jesus was not a radical, a revolutionary, a political activist, as some would have us believe. He was not a mere man who had some mystical experience that made him think he was God. He was not mixed up or confused about who He was or where He came from or what His mission was!

Jesus was more than a good man, more than a healer, more than a prophet, more than a great teacher. He was the Son of God. That's who He claimed to be. And either He told the truth or He did not. One or the other. You can't have it both ways. Either He was the Son of God, as He said He was, or He was the greatest impostor that ever lived!

But now listen. John, in this same chapter, tells us more. He says concerning Jesus, "He was in the world, and the world was made by him, and the world knew him not." John 1:10.

Not only was Jesus the Son of God. He was the world's Creator. But the world didn't recognize Him. John says in verse 3: "All things were made by him; and without him was not anything made that was made."

Too clear to be misunderstood, isn't it? And this is so important—and I'm sure so surprising to some of you—that I think we should read one or two more scriptures. The apostle Paul speaks of "God, who created all things by Jesus Christ." Ephesians 3:9.

And he says concerning Christ, "By him were all things created, that are in heaven, and that are in earth . . . all things were created by him, and for him." Colossians 1:16.

Is the picture changing for some of you? Do you see now that it isn't God the Father in the Old Testament and Jesus Christ in the New. It isn't Jesus persuading a stern, harsh, reluctant Father to be kind to us. It isn't cold legality in the Old Testament and free grace in the New. It's Jesus all the way through. And Jesus told His disciples that if they had seen Him they had seen the Father. So it's the Father all the way through. It's love all the way through!

Do you see why I say that Jesus Christ is the answer to all

our questions about our origin? He is. Because He made us!

And did you know that God, in His last message to men, a message especially for our day, over in the book of Revelation— did you know that He calls on men to worship Him as Creator? Here it is: "Fear God and give him glory . . . Worship him who made the heavens, the earth, the sea and the springs of water." Revelation 14:7, NIV.

You may have worshiped the Lord Jesus Christ as your Saviour. But now God asks you to worship Him as your Creator. They are one and the same Person. If we reject Him as Creator, we are rejecting Him as Saviour. The One who died for us is the One who made us. We can't accept Him on the cross of Calvary and reject Him in the book of Genesis!

Doesn't it put new life into the book of Genesis—when you see Jesus there?

Listen. God is Love. Jesus is Love. Our Creator is Love.

Love didn't want to wait for long ages to have the fellowship of man. Love wouldn't leave the development of man to accident and chance or the reign of fang and claw or the "survival of the fittest." Love made man on Friday of Creation week—made him in His own image—and placed him on the top of the ladder, not on the bottom rung!

And when man, by his own choice, alienated himself from his Creator—just as it says he did in the third chapter of Genesis— Love didn't let him go. Love didn't leave him to the destiny he had chosen by his act of rebellion. Love made a way. And that way was His own life!

The Son of God knew that accident and chance couldn't undo the rebellion of a moment. Time couldn't do it. Self-discipline couldn't do it. Left to himself, man would fall so far down that his bones would today be seen as those of a primitive man at the beginning of a long, long climb!

There was only one way to change man's destiny. There was only one way to give him another chance. That was to die in his place—to pay the debt that man couldn't pay. That's what the Son of God determined to do. And that's what He did!

In a book that came to my hand recently the author is writing about his family. He describes his wife as a very generous person who has a job, buys her own clothes, and has a little money left over. He says that frequently the family will want to do something that is beyond his income. He has to say, "We can't afford it." But she will say, "I'll pay the difference."

"I'll pay the difference." That's what Jesus said. Man owed a debt he couldn't pay. And Jesus said, "I'll pay the difference." But the difference was not a part of it, but all of it. Man couldn't pay anything. Calvary was God paying the difference. And the difference was His own life!

There are those who point to all the war and suffering and heartache and blame God for it—as if man were the innocent victim. But man is not the innocent victim. He is the guilty rebel. Those who shake their fists at God are blind to Calvary—and to what Calvary is all about!

Calvary proved that Jesus came not to condemn the world but to save the world. He didn't come to bring judgment but to bear judgment. He came—the innocent Lamb of God—to die for the guilty. Calvary proved that sin was the deadly, lethal thing God said it was. Calvary proved that God is love!

Those who shake their fists at God and accuse Him of being insensitive to the world's hurting, those who ask why He doesn't step in and bring an end to it all—they are blind, themselves insensitive, to the hurt in God's heart!

Think of the infinite patience and self-restraint God has shown in this whole confrontation with rebellion. Think how easy it would have been to destroy sin and sinners at the very start—before the universe had a chance to see and understand the deadly nature of rebellion.

Think how the Saviour must have longed to come and die for man as soon as he had sinned—and get it over with. Instead, He carried Calvary in His heart those thousands of years—until the time was right!

Think of the terrible temptation to come down from the cross and show men who He was—when they were saying, "Save Yourself—if You can!"

Think of the incredible patience the Saviour has shown as He has watched the suffering go on—not for one short lifetime as we watch it, but for generation after generation. How He must long to step in and stop the hurting—especially when men are saying, "If You are God, do something about it, and we'll believe You!"

But no. Our Lord has set out to save everyone He can. And He's going to do it right. He has set out to make the universe safe. And He isn't going to bungle the job with undue hurry. He will put out the fire of rebellion in a way that it will never flare up again. God is in a hurry. But He is also wise!

When I look at Calvary, I know that I take no risk when I leave my future in His hands. Nor do you!

The Search for Certainty

Not long ago a group of student leaders from across America were called to the White House. A government spokesman, in a carefully prepared speech, told them to be good students—not to bomb buildings, not to head for Morocco, not to give up on America. When he had finished, a student from Harvard stood and asked respectfully, "Sir, can you tell us on what [these] moral concepts [of yours] are founded?"

The official stood for a moment, flushed and embarrassed. Then he replied apologetically, "I'm sorry. I don't know."

You have to admire that man for being honest enough to say, "I don't know." Too many officials would have given a vague, roundabout answer that didn't say a thing.

But doesn't it make you wonder how many of our concepts today have no solid foundation? Is it possible that many of our popularly accepted beliefs are nothing but speculation?

A book familiar to all of you is Charles Darwin's *Origin of Species*. It's a book that was once called the bible of the evolutionists. It's the foundation of much that is taught in our schools today.

The other day someone remarked that Darwin's book is full of words that indicate vague uncertainty about the views it presents. We've known this all along, of course. But it sounded like something interesting to follow up; so I asked someone to make an informal tabulation.

Now naturally the tabulation is not completely accurate. The book was not fed into a computer, so undoubtedly some words and phrases have been missed. But where the figures are off, they're off on the conservative side. I thought you'd be interested in what was discovered. For instance, thirty-six times the author says, "I think" or "we may think." And thirty-nine times he says, "I believe." Here is just a portion of the tabulation:

36 I think
    we may think

39 I believe

11 good reason to believe

16 inclined to believe

16 on my view
    our view
    general view
    adopt this view

9 we may suppose
   I may suppose

11 must suppose
    then suppose
    we suppose
    to suppose

5 supposed

9 will tend
   may tend

12 it appears

25 we may infer
    to safely infer
    I infer

11 seems to me

18 may conclude
    led me to conclude
    safely concluded

10 in all probability
    the probability
    some probability

87 probably

51 probable

10 might have
    might have been

13 is possible

6 I suspect

7 been assumed
   I have assumed

6 apparently

Interestingly, instead of using a single word, Darwin often expressed his uncertainty in long phrases such as these:

as far as our ignorance permits us to judge
as far as I can discover
dare not assert positively
not pretend to conjecture
if my theory be true
difficult to come to any conclusions
doubtfully inclined to believe
although we are ignorant
if I do not greatly deceive myself

There are at least eight hundred of these indications of uncertainty throughout the book—often half a dozen at a single page opening!

Tell me. How long would you stay with an insurance company that worded its policies like that? Would you sign a contract—worded like that?

Have you actually read Darwin's book? Probably you haven't. But at least you know that for more than a century it has been accepted by millions as containing the classic explanation of our origins. And yet eight hundred times the author is saying "I don't know"—or its equivalent!

Doesn't it shake you up just a little to realize that a book so widely accepted should be so filled with uncertainty? Doesn't it frighten you a little to think how shaky a foundation the book is—for anybody's faith? Doesn't it make you long for something more solid, more secure, more worthy of our trust? It should!

You see, it's so easy for us to put science on a pedestal and forget that there are some things science cannot do. We forget that, especially when it comes to the distant past, science has very few facts to work with. Scientists do the best they can with the facts they have. But it's easy to forget that a great deal of what the scientists tell us is not fact at all. Rather, it is their interpretation of the facts.

This is why so many people have the impression that there is a conflict between science and religion. Actually there is no conflict at all about the existing facts. The controversy concerns only the interpretation of the facts. And the trouble is that the interpretation may be based entirely on unproven assumptions.

For instance, fossils are found in rocks, and they are found in a certain order. These are facts. But what does that order mean? An answer to that is interpretation.

Let's say that some bones are found, evidently belonging to a human skeleton. They appear to be very old. A scientist becomes interested and attempts a reconstruction of the skeleton to which they belonged. He doesn't have all the bones, you understand. So he has to fill in with his imagination. I think you see that some mistakes can be made.

And then suppose an attempt is made to fill out that skeleton, to put flesh on the bones. Do you realize that two different scientists might come up with vastly different results? The resulting reconstruction can hardly be called science. It depends too much on the scientist's preconceived opinions. The same bones could be fitted together, filled out with speculation, and made to appear very, very old—or very modern. Do you see?

I want to give you an illustration from the field of archaeology. Archaeologists, it seems, are always digging up broken pottery. They piece it together and date ancient cultures by the style of the pottery left behind. And in general they do pretty well.

But I want you to see that there is more than one way to put a vase together. And for this illustration I am indebted to my friend Dr. Leonard Brand, who is chairman of the biology department of the graduate school at Loma Linda University.

Let's suppose, he says, that an archaeologist named William is digging in the ruins of an ancient city. He finds several pieces of glass, and they look as if they might be part of a broken vase. That's all he has—just some pieces of broken glass. (See Figure 1.)

So if William wants to know what the vase looked like, he will have to fill in with his imagination. It won't be like putting a jigsaw puzzle together, when you have all the pieces. William *doesn't have* all the pieces.

So he does the best he can. He uses all his background in

Figure 1   **Figure 2**

archaeology, all his knowledge of ancient cultures. And he comes up with a reconstruction (Figure 2), the way he thinks the vase looked. The dark pieces are the pieces he found. The white is his imagination.

Or put it this way. The pieces of glass are his facts. The white is his interpretation of the facts. No one will question his facts. But someone may question his interpretation.

Let's say that somebody does. Let's say that another archaeologist named Margaret comes along. She thinks his interpretation is wrong. She thinks the vase should be taller. And she thinks it should have two ridges instead of one. She makes a reconstruction that looks different—using the same pieces of glass, the same facts, you understand. (Figure 3.)

Now we have two interpretations of the same facts. Which one is right? You really can't tell, without more facts.

So let's say that they keep looking and they find two more pieces of glass. One piece fits Margaret's idea, but not Williams's. The other piece doesn't fit either one. So they have to revise their ideas, and together they come up with another reconstruction. (Figure 4.)

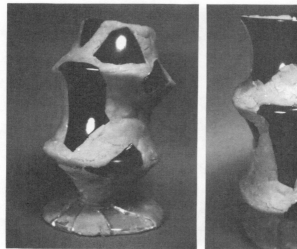

Figure 3

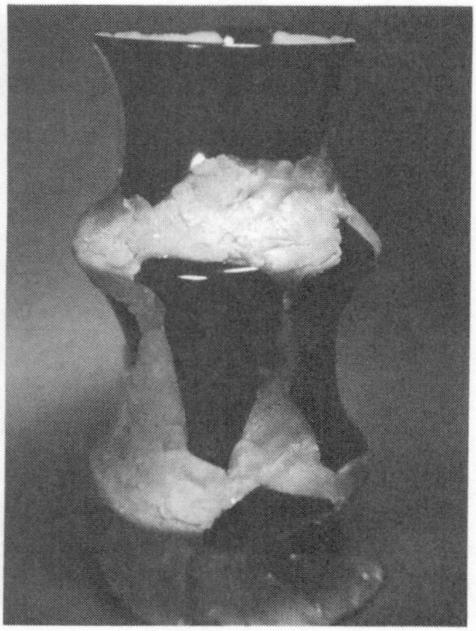

Figure 4

Figure 5

Now can we be sure that this is how the original vase looked? No, we can't. There are too many pieces still missing. So we still have only an interpretation.

But in this case it just happens that we have the original vase. So we can *see* how it looked. (Figure 5.) Finding more facts did help. But there was still a lot of speculation.

You see, if you don't have all the facts you have to use a lot of imagination. You have to put the pieces of a broken vase together the best you can. That's all you can do. *Unless you happen to know its maker.* Unless you know the creator—and he tells you how he made it!

When it comes to the distant past, we don't have all the pieces. We don't have all the facts. The complete set of facts can't be assembled by any tool of science. And none of us were there when this world was made.

The only way we can be sure about how this world was made is to take the word of the One who says He made it. Otherwise, we're left largely to speculation. And our speculations aren't very solid. They have a way of letting us down. One theory gives way, and we jump onto another. We're forever revising our ideas.

Our universities, our great institutions of learning, are a source of much enlightenment. Yet in some areas they deal very little with certainties. Physics and mathematics, of course, are exact sciences. But there are fields of study in which, it must be admitted, much theory and conjecture are taught. Graduates come away with degrees. But some of them come away with less than certainty.

The result of all this? Restlessness. Never has a generation been so restless. Men and women are shuffling from theory to theory, from speculation to speculation, from cult to cult, trying to find some meaning in life, some reason for existence, some hope. And finding none, they continue the trek to anywhere or nowhere.

Men and women are knocking on the wall of the unseen world, wondering what is on the other side. They are sitting on hillsides, watching strange lights bobbing in the sky, wondering why they are so elusive. They are turning to the astrology columns, trying to find some comfort, some security, in the stars. Millions are following psychic predictions to dead ends—and reeling in their disillusionment.

A decade or two ago men demanded some reason and logic in their beliefs. Today millions turn to the wildest speculation and sheerest nonsense. Some decide that we are all robots, manipulated by some sort of cosmic energy. Others confuse the evils with the acts of God and lump them all together. They decide that the universe, if it is ruled at all, must be ruled by an uncaring crackpot—or at best by a mathematical equation!

And there isn't a breath of hope in it all. Nothing to catch hold of. Nothing to tell us who we are—or why. The feelings of millions today are expressed in the words of Edna St. Vincent Millay:

Life must go on,
I forget just why.

Yes, ours is a generation that is crying out, "I don't know." But wanting desperately to find the answers. Wanting to know who we are and where we came from—and why!

Today a great many adopted children, now adults, are spending large amounts of time and money and patience, trying to discover who their real parents are. They want to know their real identity.

And now, on a national level, we have already spent huge amounts of money trying to find out who our cosmic parents might be, trying to discover if we are alone in the universe. The Viking project alone cost us a billion dollars.

Is it worth it? True, we have broken the shackles that tie us to this planet. We have launched our ships in the cosmic ocean, and we have learned to sail. Our space missions have been a triumph of technology.

But the real message of Viking, and of all our space missions, is "I don't know." That's the cry of this lonely planet. And the dollars we have spent are a measure of the desperateness of our search for the answers.

But do we really have to spend that much to find them? Has the Creator of our world and of man mischievously hidden the secrets of the universe in the soil of the planet Mars?

Friend, are you tired of the restlessness, tired of the uncertainty, tired of not knowing anything for sure?

I suppose that if someone like Charles Darwin had written the book of Genesis, it might begin something like this:

"It is speculated that in the beginning God *may have more or less* created the heaven and *possibly* the earth. The earth was *probably* without form, and it *must have been* dark on the face of the deep.

"Some have conjectured that the Spirit of God *just may have* moved upon the face of the waters. And *somebody must surely have said,* 'Let there be light.' Or it *may have been* some chemical reaction that we don't understand. Obviously light appeared from somewhere."

But enough of that! Two paragraphs are enough! Aren't you glad that Charles Darwin didn't write the book of Genesis?

Thank God it doesn't read that way! Thank God the author of Genesis didn't have the slightest doubt about the accuracy of what He was writing! Listen. Drink it in like sparkling spring water. Let it refresh your soul!

"In the beginning God created the heaven and the earth. And the earth was without form, and void; and darkness was upon the face of the deep. And the Spirit of God moved upon the face of the waters.

"And God said, Let there be light: and there was light. And God saw the light, that it was good: and God divided the light from the darkness. And God called the light Day, and the darkness he called Night. And the evening and the morning were the first day.

"And God said, Let there be a firmament in the midst of the waters, and let it divide the waters from the waters. . . . And God called the firmament Heaven. And the evening and the morning were the second day. . . .

"And God called the dry land Earth . . . And God said, Let the earth bring forth grass, the herb yielding seed, and the fruit tree yielding fruit after his kind . . . and it was so. . . . And the evening and the morning were the third day. . . .

"And God made two great lights; the greater light to rule the day, and the lesser light to rule the night: he made the stars also. . . . and God saw that it was good. And the evening and the morning were the fourth day. . . .

"And God created great whales, and every living creature that moveth . . . and God saw that it was good. . . . And the evening and the morning were the fifth day. . . .

"And God said, Let us make man in our image, after our likeness: and let them have dominion over . . . all the earth . . . So God created man in his own image, in the image of God created he him; male and female created he them. . . . And God saw every thing that he had made, and . . . it was very good. And the evening and the morning were the sixth day.

"Thus the heavens and the earth were finished, and all the host of them. And on the seventh day God ended his work which he had made; and he rested on the seventh day from all his work which he had made."

Don't you like that? Don't you like the solid sound of it, the certainty of it, the secure feeling it gives you?

Listen, friend. The only uncertainties in the Bible have to do with man's decisions. God made man with the power of choice. And He'll never violate that freedom. He'll never invade the sacred precincts of the soul where a man decides.

You'll find the word "if" in the Bible many times. But the "ifs" have to do with men, not with God. They have to do with men's decisions. With yours and mine. Men and women, you and I—we are the only uncertainties in God's book!

Wouldn't you like to remove the uncertainty, just now, about what your decision will be?

Darwin's Dilemma

Anna was only four years old the night Fynn* found her on the fog-shrouded London docks. Fynn was six feet two and 225 pounds. She wouldn't tell him where she lived, but announced that she was coming home to live with him. So he took her home. His mother was used to taking in strays—whether dogs or cats or people.

But little did Fynn know how this tiny child would dominate his life. At four she possessed an irresistible charm. And already she had a very special acquaintance with "Mister God." But by the time she was six she was a theologian, a mathematician, and certainly a philosopher. Fynn considered himself well educated, but when he tried to answer Anna's questions he found himself continually going to the foot of the class.

One evening they were sitting on the railway wall, watching the trains go by. Anna was drinking lemonade. Suddenly she started to giggle. She giggled until she got the hiccups. When finally she had settled back to normal, Fynn asked her what was so funny.

"Well," she said, "I just thought I could answer a squillion questions." *Squillion* was a word she had invented for numbers too big to express any other way.

"Me too," Fynn said, not surprised at all.

Anna leaned forward excited. "Can you do it too?"

---

*The material here is taken from *Mister God, This is Anna* by Fynn. Copyright © 1974 by Fynn. Reprinted by permission of Holt, Rinehart, and Winston, Publishers.

7—T.O.P.

"Sure," he said. "Nothing to it. Mind you, I might get about half a squillion wrong."

She was disappointed. "Oh, I get all my answers right."

This was going too far. A little correction was in order. He said firmly, "You can't. Nobody can answer a squillion questions right." "I can," she said. "I can answer a squillion squillion questions right."

"That's just not possible. Nobody can do that."

"I can—I really can."

Fynn was ready to scold her. He turned her to face him. But he was met by a pair of eyes that were calm and certain. "I can teach you," she said.

And before he could say another word she was off.

"What's one add one add one?"

"Three, of course."

"What's one add two?"

"Three."

"What's eight take away five?"

"Still three." Where was she leading him?

"What's eight take away six add one?"

"Three."

"What's a hundred and three take away a hundred?"

"Hold it," he said. "Of course that answer's three, but you're cheating a bit, aren't you?"

"No, I'm not."

"Why, you could go on asking that kind of question until the cows come home."

At that Anna exploded into a roar of laughter, and he wondered what he had said that was so funny. Then he realized that asking questions till the cows come home was certainly the same as asking a squillion questions!

But she turned the thumbscrew one more turn. "What's a half and a half and a half and a—" He put his hand over her mouth. He didn't need to answer. He had the message.

She finished off with, "And how many question sums is *three* the answer to?"

Duly chastised, he answered, "Squillions."

He turned away to watch the trains. And after a moment or

two she put her head on his shoulder and said, "Isn't it funny, Fynn; every number is the answer to squillions of questions!"

That was the beginning of a game they would play for many months. Start with the answer. Find the question. Any number, any sentence, anything you could say was the answer to something. For Fynn it was not only a game, but an education in reverse. He had been taught the old-fashioned way—question first, answer second. But this tiny redhead was teaching him a new approach. She was teaching him to walk backward until at last he bumped into the question!

Walking backward, of course, is not always the safest way to proceed!

But Anna's game is not really new. The advocates of evolution have been playing it for many years now. In the supposed magic of long ages in the past they have found an answer that they like, and they start from there. Like Anna, they proceed not from the question to the answer, but starting with the answer they try to find questions that fit.

Am I overstating the case? I think not. Evolution is definitely based upon assumptions. And those assumptions have never been proved. Evolution assumes (1) that nature has always behaved just as it does now, and (2) that the uniform action of nature has never been interrupted by catastrophe.

In other words, evolution has an answer it likes, and is trying to make the questions, and the facts, fit its answer!

Wouldn't it be better—and easier too—to take the clear, simple, plain, understandable statement of Genesis that "in the beginning God created the heaven and the earth"? Genesis 1:1.

Over and over, in the Scriptures, God identifies Himself as the One who made all things, who made the heaven and the earth. In contrast, He speaks of "the gods that have not made the heavens and the earth." Jeremiah 10:11.

He asks, "Is there any god beside me, or any creator, even one that I do not know?" Isaiah 44:8, NEB.

He throws out a challenge to all false gods: " 'Present your case,' the Lord says. 'Bring forward your strong arguments,' the King of Jacob says." Isaiah 41:21, NASB.

The gods of accident and chance, along with the gods of wood and stone, have a standing invitation to demonstrate their creative power. They are said to have performed wonderful feats of change, of evolutionary progress, in the distant past. But nobody can get them to perform now. Even on the darkest nights, even in the most isolated wilderness, in tropical heat or arctic cold, where it is wet or where it is dry, in the air or under the sea—cats have not been turning into dogs, or robins into sea gulls!

It reminds me of one of the many court cases in the controversy over Alexander Graham Bell's right to telephone patents. On this occasion lawyers brought into court a model of the 1860 Reis machine—a German inventor's device that just missed being a telephone. They hoped to demonstrate in court that the Reis machine could "talk" and that therefore the Bell patents were not valid. To the courtroom's amusement, however, experts tried in vain to get the device to perform. It would squeak, but it wouldn't speak. And one lawyer explained in desperation, "It *can* speak, but it won't!"

That's the dilemma of the advocates of evolution. Their theory *has* worked, they tell us. But it won't!

The truth is that Darwinism has been in trouble for some time now. Things haven't been going well at all for its promoters. Says Tom Bethell, writing in *Harper's* magazine, "Darwin, I suggest, is in the process of being discarded, but perhaps in deference to the venerable old gentleman, resting comfortably in Westminster Abbey next to Sir Isaac Newton, it is being done as discreetly and gently as possible, with a minimum of publicity."

A Harvard-trained lawyer has written a book called *Darwin Retried*.

Creationists are insisting that evolution be presented in the schools as a theory rather than a fact, and that the Genesis account of creation be placed alongside it, so that students know they have a choice.

Yes, Darwin is in trouble. More and more scientists are realizing that the concepts of the evolution theory are just too unreasonable. They are realizing that it is simply impossible for intelligent life, or any life at all, to have evolved from nothing.

Actually, Darwinism, in its original form, has long been

dead. We know now that the variations we see in species are strictly limited by the genetic information stored by each biological kind. These variations could never be a means of producing new kinds. The latest discoveries in the field of genetics, rather than supporting evolution of new kinds, are the most powerful evidence which has yet emerged against the whole theory.

There is very little comfort for the evolutionist in the study of DNA. The truth is that the new biology has raised more questions than it has answered. Scientists are baffled as to how the simplest organic molecules came into existence in the first place. And still more baffling is how proteins and genes got together in the first cells. The chances against it are tremendous.

The science of genetics, you see, shows how changes may occur by the assortment and recombination of genes; but these changes concern only minor features such as color, shape, or size of parts. The major features that distinguish one kind from another, as a cat from a dog or a lily from a rose, have never been known to change. They are fixed.

Now let me say this right here. Darwin was not wrong in everything that he taught. Some features of his work were correct. He showed that variation does take place in all organisms, and that these variations are the basis for the great bulk of the species now known. Today the cataloged species of animals number about a million and a half, and there are almost half a million species of plants.

But here is where Darwin made his mistake. He attempted to account for not only the species but all the larger categories too—the families, the orders, the classes. In trying to do this, in trying to make the facts fit an assumption, he went deeply into vague speculation, and led the world into a belief in organic evolution—a concept that scientists have found impossible adequately to prove.

Actually, the variation that we see within the kinds of animals, the evidence of adaptation, rather than being the result of organic evolution, is evidence of the Creator's power and forethought and care for His creatures. Let me explain.

You recall that God, when He had finished creating our

world and all that was in it, found it "very good." Everything He had created was very good, perfect, with no need to adapt. But when sin came in, all was changed. The environment, the climate—all underwent change, sometimes drastic change. So what did a loving Creator do? Did He leave the creatures He had made with no defense against these new, and often unpleasant, conditions? No. He gave them the ability to adapt. But that does not mean that He gave bears the ability to become leopards, or horses to become lions, worms to become robins, or gorillas to become men. Do you see?

Evolution, I say again, is in trouble. No matter how enthusiastically it tries to sell its speculations, something in nature keeps standing up and saying No!

For instance, one of the most puzzling problems in the theory of evolution is that the vertebrate animals have no ancestral roots!

The animal kingdom, as you know, is divided into two major groups—the vertebrates and the invertebrates, those that have a backbone and those that do not. If the theory of evolution is true, then there must be a bridge between the groups. Somewhere among the invertebrates we must find an ancestor of the vertebrates. Many guesses have been made, but in every case the structure of the two forms of life is so different that ancestry would be completely impossible.

Some evolutionists suggest that vertebrates originated in the annelids, the group to which the earthworm belongs. An early worm, according to this theory, many millions of years ago gave rise to a creature that, after millions of generations, became a robin.

But any such succession would require such a complete rearrangement of anatomy that it is out of the question. The robin says, "No! No roots!"

And then there's the matter of time. Time is something the evolutionists seem to have plenty of. They add or subtract a few billion years without batting an eye. Supposedly anything can happen—if you just give it enough time.

But take a sea gull. How long would it take to produce a sea gull by the process of evolution—if it could be done at all?

Evolutionists usually speculate that life began in a primitive "soup" of simple molecules that formed by chance. And these simple molecules randomly combined until by luck they formed a large complex molecule that could play an important role in a living cell. And ultimately life began. That's what they say.

But recently even some evolutionary scientists have begun to wonder. They wonder if life really did begin that way.

You see, a simple protein molecule might contain thirty amino acids joined together end to end in a single line. But that isn't so simple, because there are about twenty different types of amino acids, any one of which could occupy any or all of the thirty positions. If just one amino acid is out of position you're in trouble.

How many different protein molecules are possible? Well, begin with this. What chance would you have of flipping a coin thirty times and having it land heads up every time? Less than one chance in a billion.

But now just suppose that the coin you are flipping has not two sides but twenty sides. Flip it thirty times. What chance would you have of getting it to show a specific side all thirty times? You'd have one chance in a number with thirty-nine zeros!

In other words, that many different kinds of protein molecules would be possible. And you have to have the right one. How long would evolutionary life have to wait to even get started? A physical chemist has figured that it would probably take more than two billion years just to get the right molecule!

I won't weary you with all the calculations. But that's only a single molecule. Yet a living cell contains more than a thousand different kinds of protein molecules. And in addition it has thousands of equally complex nucleic acid molecules (DNA), fats, carbohydrates, and many, many other kinds of molecules. Just in one living cell. Is your head reeling a little?

So how long would it take to make a sea gull? If life developed by chance alone, it would take about 100,000,000,000,000,000, 000,000,000,000,000,000,000,000,000 years just to produce a sea gull—to say nothing of a man! Maybe we need Anna's word "squillions" after all!

And the dilemma for the evolutionist is that he insists the world is only about four and a half billion years old. Not enough time! And that's embarrassing for, of all people, an evolutionist!

But now listen. If life originated in the sea at all, as the evolutionists tell us it did, you have to have a very, very old ocean. But what if the ocean isn't even a billion years old? What if the ocean can be shown to be relatively youthful—say not more than 10,000 years old? What then?

The evolutionist says that for a period of at least a billion years the ocean has remained at roughly constant salinity while evolution was taking place.

On the other hand, the creationist thinks of the ocean in the time-frame of not more than ten thousand years. The book of Genesis tells us that the earth in its original condition was covered with water (Genesis 1:2). But later God formed the ocean basins by gathering the waters together, allowing the dry land to appear (Genesis 1:9). The ocean again covered the entire earth during the global Flood in the days of Noah. After the Flood the ocean returned to its present basins.

Two views, wide apart. But what does the ocean say? What is the witness of the sea?

Careful study of present erosion and sedimentation rates— we shall not go into detail—has turned up some facts that may surprise you.

For instance, a total of 27.5 billion tons of sediment are delivered to the ocean every year. (To make that figure more understandable, let us say that eighty train cars of sediment are being added to the ocean every second!) Most evolutionary uniformitarian geologists would admit that this total is approximately correct.

So we ask, How long would it take to deliver the present continents to the ocean if the present rate of erosion should continue? The answer, skipping over the calculations, is that the continents are being denuded at a rate that could level them in a mere 50 million years! Yet evolutionary uniformitarian geologists feel certain that the continents have existed for at least a billion years. Think it through. During that supposed billion years our present continents could have been completely eroded more than 20 times! Yet the continents are still here. And they don't appear to have been eroded away even once— yet!

I won't weary you with more figures. Let me simply say that the testimony of the ocean can only be embarrassing to the evolutionist. The ocean, like the sea gull and the robin, and like all nature, stands up and says a fearless No!

Is it any wonder that evolutionary scientists in increasing numbers are adjusting their position?

Listen to this from Isaac Asimov, writing in the September, 1977, issue of the *Saturday Evening Post* on the subject of DNA research. "Evolution," he says, "has always worked blindly, depending on whatever mutations happened to occur, and on whatever environmental conditions did to make some mutations more successful than others ('natural selection').

"Human beings, however, *can substitute intelligent direction for chance*. Scientists can, in effect, create their own mutations, eventually design specific mutations, and then decide which mutations might be worth encouraging into continued existence." (Emphasis ours.)

What do you think of that? Are scientists coming around to admit that a little intelligent direction might help—that intelligent direction is better than chance? Why not come all the way around to the book of Genesis, to believing that God in the beginning, by His intelligent direction, by simply speaking the word, created the heaven and the earth?

Isn't that easier than believing that life, unaided by intelligence, could arise from lifelessness?

Yes, evolution has been playing Anna's game. It has the answer it likes, but it can't seem to find the questions to fit. Is it any wonder that a lot of people, some scientists among them, are getting tired of the game?

Love Is Something You Do

May I take you to Old Palestine, the land where Jesus walked?

If you should set out to walk from Jerusalem to Jericho, you would be vividly aware of just one direction—*down*. The two cities are only twenty miles apart. But Jerusalem is high on a mountain ridge, its elevation 2500 feet above sea level. Jericho is 820 feet below sea level in the Jordan Valley. What a drop— about 3300 feet in so short a distance!

The Jericho Road isn't one you'd want to travel every day. Nor was it in the time of Christ. I have been on it several times. To make it easier to travel, whether going down or going up, the road was constructed with switchback after switchback. And these tortuous turns, along with the hills and gullies beside the road, made it easy for robbers to hide.

Jesus told a story one day—a story about a certain man who was going *down* from Jerusalem to Jericho. And you know now what Jesus meant by *down*.

As the traveler made his way down the treacherous road, it was necessary to pass through a portion of the wilderness of Judea. The road led through a wild and rocky ravine which was infested by robbers. Here he was attacked, stripped of everything valuable, beaten, and left beside the road to die.

Now what would happen? Who would show concern for this poor man, beaten and bleeding? All heaven watched to see.

First a priest came along, but he merely glanced at the wounded man. Then came a Levite. He was curious and stopped to see what had happened. He knew what he should do, but he didn't want to do it. He wished he hadn't come that way. He persuaded himself that the poor man's plight was no concern of his. And besides, what if he were a Samaritan?

But along the road came one of those hated Samaritans. He didn't stop to question whether the wounded man was Jew or Gentile. He didn't stop to think that he himself might be in danger in this deserted place. Someone was in trouble, and that was enough.

He took off his own cloak to cover the victim. He gave him first aid as best he could and refreshed him with provisions intended for his own journey. He lifted him onto his own animal and proceeded slowly so as not to cause him more pain. He took him to an inn and cared for him tenderly through the night.

In the morning, seeing that the injured man was much improved, he left him in the care of the innkeeper, paid for his lodging, and promised to take care of any additional expense when next he should stop at the inn.

That was the story. What would you have done if you had passed that way?

Love is not just something to talk about. Love is something we do. We measure *God's love for us* by looking at Calvary. And God measures *our love for Him* by looking at the Jericho Road!

He looks at the Jericho Road. And if neither He nor His angel watchers can find the slightest evidence that we have been there, a single life we have touched, one lone tear that we have dried, even one hurt that we have healed—if instead of the Jericho Road we have chosen the high-speed freeway that bypasses the world's need—then how can either God or man say that we have loved at all?

Love is something we do. The Christian life is not a dreamlike drift toward heaven. You and I, whether we want to be or not, are involved in the great controversy between good and evil. And there's no such thing as sitting back in some neutral corner and letting God and Satan fight it out!

The Lord Jesus, as this controversy winds up, wants to use you and me as exhibits of His power to transform lives. He wants to make us winsome demonstrations of His love. What

kind of exhibit, what kind of demonstration have we been today? Is it any wonder that angels weep at our lack of compassion? Is it surprising that all heaven is shocked at our indiffer-
ence?

Who of us cares enough to listen to the heartbeat of despair?
Who of us stops to feel the dwindling pulse of hope? We don't
need miracle drugs to treat the wounds of the soul. We need
miracle people. The heartbreak of the world is the heartbreak
of Jesus. And it ought to be ours!

It is a terrible thing to assume that heaven is our destination
while we bypass the Jericho Road. It is a delusion to rest satisfied with our degrees for the mind while our hearts have never
been educated.

Is it possible that we are allowing the corruption around us to
drive all the compassion out of our hearts? True. It's revolting.
But can the violence in our streets ever excuse us for letting
compassion die a violent death in our hearts?

The late Moshe Dayan, soldier par excellence that he was,
had a great deal of compassion for the Arab people. He invited
to his wedding an Arab who had once tried to kill him. On another occasion some Arabs came up to a checkpoint with a cart
of fruit carefully arranged for market. The inspectors dug into
it, looking for weapons, and left it in disarray. Moshe Dayan
severely reprimanded them for their insensitiveness.

Love, if it is love at all, will be seen on the Jericho Road. It
will be seen in the marketplace. It will be seen in the church.
What did the apostle James say about a faith that is not demonstrated?

"What does it profit, my brethren, if someone says he has
faith but does not have works? Can faith save him? If a brother
or sister is naked and destitute of daily food, and one of you says
to them, 'Depart in peace, be warmed and filled,' but you do not
give them the things which are needed for the body, what does
it profit? Thus also faith by itself, if it does not have works, is
dead." James 2:14-17, NKJV.

It's a strange faith that sits by and does nothing. True, we are
not saved by works. We are not saved by anything we can do.
But what we do is an indicator of what we are. Our actions ei-

ther authenticate the genuineness of our commitment to Christ—or they betray our hypocrisy. One or the other.

Jesus was repeatedly puzzled and disappointed by the inconsistency of those who claimed to love Him. And it is no different today. Notice three brief but disturbing sentences from Jesus.

"If you love Me, keep My commandments." John 14:15, NKJV.

Another time He said it this way:

"You are My friends if you do whatever I command you." John 15:14, NKJV.

And then catch the hurt in these words of Jesus:

"But why do you call Me 'Lord, Lord,' and do not do the things which I say?" Luke 6:46.

You've seen these bumper stickers that say, "Honk if you love Jesus." Well, there was one that was different. It said, "If you love Jesus, pay tithe. Anybody can honk!"

Yes, anybody can honk. Anybody can hold up a placard that says, "I believe in Jesus." But our Lord is waiting for something more than that. And He has a right to expect it.

The trouble is that *behavior* is not very popular today. Rather, the mood of this generation is feeling, sensitivity, and the inevitable love—with as many definitions as there are definers. But what we need are some absolutes. We need the Ten Commandments to define how love should act.

Lloyd John Ogilvie said it so well:

"Take him in! Accept him as the greatest *man* who ever lived! Revere him as the most penetrating psychologist who ever analyzed life. Mark the calendar B.C. and A.D. Plan your customs around his birth, death, and resurrection. Speak of the gentle Jesus, meek and mild. Paint portraits of him, write the libraries full of line and verse about him. Sing for him; preach about him. We will have done everything we can with human skill and duration—except one—made him the absolute Lord of our lives!"

Don't you like that? Yes, we're willing to put Jesus on a golden pedestal. But we don't want Him on the throne!

Consistency has been called a jewel. And certainly it's a rare jewel—one far too seldom seen!

Seven men were working side by side in the blazing sun, hoeing long rows across a huge plot of land. The boss would return at evening to inspect their work. C. V. Garnett, writing in *Insight* magazine, tells the story.

At noon the men exchanged their hoes for lunch pails and found some shade. As the others began eating, a gray-haired man—they called him Old Lew—dropped to one knee and bowed his head. They were used to this ritual and paid no attention. All too soon the half hour allotted for lunch was over, and Old Lew rose to go.

"Sit down, Lew. It's too hot to be hurrying out there," said Dan. "The boss'll never know the difference if we take an extra fifteen minutes."

"You men do what you want," said Old Lew. And he stepped out into the sun.

When he was gone, Dan shook his head. "I don't get it. What difference would a few extra minutes make, anyhow?"

"To him, plenty. An honest day's work is part of his religion, part of him." It was Young Lew who had spoken up. They called him Young Lew to distinguish him from the older man.

And now it was Dan again. "Look, you don't have to stick up for him just because you're courting his daughter. The way I look at it, we work because we got to. So if you can go easy on yourself, who's it hurt?"

"It would hurt him," Young Lew tried to explain. "The agreement was for a half-hour lunch."

"I don't trust him and that crazy religion of his," said Dan.

But Bill disagreed. "He's OK. He don't bother nobody."

And now Rube spoke up. "I admire him. If only he didn't have that funny religion."

And Young Lew said, "Wait a minute! What makes him the man you admire *is* his religion. You can't have it both ways."

Well, maybe it was to ease the tension that Tom Wilson came up with a joke he'd heard the night before. That reminded Bill of one, and Rube told his favorite. The time was forgotten.

Suddenly Rube shouted, "Hey! Look at the time!"

The men leaped to their feet and began running toward the field. "That old man will be across the field and back," Dan shouted.

"The boss will know we've been goofing off," called another.

"The old man will probably tell him." That was from Dan.

But Young Lew said, "He won't have to tell him. Our rows will tell the story."

They raced on together. In the distance they could see Old Lew, bent over his hoe. Then, as they neared the field, suddenly they stopped. There, just as they had expected, Old Lew's row was a long way ahead of where it was before lunch. *But the other six rows were all even with his!*

They couldn't believe what they saw. But when they saw the old man step from one row to the next, they knew it was true. He had been stepping from one row to another, keeping each man's row even with his own!

What a sermon! A sermon preached by a man with a hoe!

Friend, what if the love of God for us had been all talk and no action? What if Jesus had not bothered to come and die for us? What if He had cast us off like broken toys—and made new men and women in our place?

What if He had wept divine tears over our plight—and sent us messages filled with pathos, eloquent in their sympathy for our fallen condition? But nothing more.

What if He had stepped out on a cloud and punctuated His pledge of love with celestial fireworks—and never followed up? What if He had come as far as Calvary—and decided it was more important to save Himself than to save us?

We sing about the love of God—and how it would take a great scroll and an ocean filled with ink to tell it. But have you ever thought how dark this world would be if Calvary had never happened? Just the scroll—stretched from sky to sky?

Thank God that isn't the way it is!

But what about *our* love—our commitment to Him? Is it all words—and nothing more?

Many have thought that once we accept Christ there is nothing more to do—that at the time of conversion we are saved once for all, and that nothing we do or don't do in the future can possibly change our status of being saved.

But is it true? Does conversion, no matter how sincere, take away our power of choice? What if a man makes a sincere commitment to Christ today, but tomorrow or next week or next year changes his mind and enters the service of Satan? What if today a man wants to be saved, but somewhere down in the future decides he *doesn't* want to be saved? Will God save him anyway—against his will?

Think again of Jesus. What if He had decided to die in our place—and then decided not to? Would we be saved anyway—because once He had intended to save us?

The apostle Paul had a very remarkable conversion. Was it impossible, then, for him to lose out—after the Damascus Road experience and after all his preaching?

"I discipline my body and bring it into subjection, lest, when I have preached to others, I myself should become disqualified." 1 Corinthians 9:27, NKJV.

Paul disqualified? He knew that it *could* happen!

How did Jesus indicate that it is possible for converted people to backslide and eventually be lost? "He who endures to the end shall be saved." Matthew 24:13, NKJV.

And twice in the book of Revelation our Lord makes it clear that the crown is only for those who endure to the end. "Be faithful unto death, and I will give you the crown of life." Revelation 2:10, last part, NKJV. "Behold, I come quickly! Hold fast what you have, that no one may take your crown." Revelation 3:11, NKJV.

Evidently a decision for Christ does not take away a man's power to choose. His decision can be reversed. It is not a matter of once-saved-always-saved. Judas decided to join up with Christ. He was the most brilliant of the disciples, and his companions were proud that he was one of them. But he ended up betraying his Lord. Will he be saved because he was once one of the Twelve?

Evidently faith needs to be demonstrated. Obedience may not be popular, but it is important. A person who loves his Lord will delight to obey Him.

But why is it that thousands of Christians—very sincere Christians—are living such humdrum lives? How is it that they have managed to miss the miracle? They have kept the commandments—or tried to. They know their Bibles. They know truth from error. They consider themselves converted. They work hard for the Lord. But they have no living, breathing, personal relationship with Him.

And why is it that thousands who *want* to keep the commandments, and *try to*, seem not to be *able to*? They are often defeated—helpless before the attacks of the enemy. There is no power in their lives. And they are bewildered. They are stunned. Doesn't Christianity work, after all?

Thousands have made a sincere commitment to Christ. They have experienced the new birth. They are elated by the assurance that their sins are pardoned. They are exhilarated by the new life. They live for months on miracle clouds. And then they fall off. What is wrong? Does God work a miracle at the beginning of the new life—and then leave us to struggle and blunder on our own and fail in the end? Something is wrong!

This may shock you. But forgiveness, costly as it is, wonderful as it is—*forgiveness is not enough.* If the gospel of Christ offers nothing more than forgiveness, it is a defective gospel. And if Jesus can give us a miracle boost at the beginning of the way but is unable to make any *continuing* provision to free us from the power of sin, He might just as well not have come to earth at all!

Did Jesus make such a mistake? Did He intend only to forgive us and get us started right—and then leave us on our own, still the slaves of sin, still powerless to break its hold upon us?

No, He didn't!

We desperately need pardon. We need to be born again. But also, and just as desperately, we need the power to stop sinning. *The pardon and the power.* Could Jesus provide one but not the other? Did He forget about the power? Is He able to forgive our past, but unable to change us, to fit us for the future life?

No, says the apostle Paul.

"I am not ashamed of the gospel of Christ, for it is the power of God to salvation for everyone who believes, for the Jew first and also for the Greek." Romans 1:16, NKJV.

No, says the apostle Jude.

"Now to Him who is able to keep you from stumbling, and to present you faultless before the presence of His glory with exceeding joy." Jude 24, NKJV.

And no, says the apostle Peter.

"Who are kept by the power of God through faith for salvation ready to be revealed in the last time." 1 Peter 1:5, NKJV.

The power is there. But it is the power of God. Not our power. Not willpower. Not self-discipline. The source of power is outside ourselves. It is something that God does for us. The Christian life all the way through—*not just at the beginning*—is a miracle of God's power.

We should have known that we would fail—struggling along on our own, trying to polish up the outside while we were mocked by what we knew about the inside. We should have known. Because of what Jesus said.

"Without Me you can do nothing." John 15:5, NKJV.

But sometimes the words don't register until we need them desperately. *Then* they shine like the sun. *Then* we see that we have been trying to do what only God can do!

Yet strangely enough, this rock-bottom experience, this discouragement and despair over our repeated defeat—this seems to be a part of the process, a part of the way God saves us.

Why? Because we are not ready for the wonder of what *God* can do until we are convinced of the utter futility of what *we* can do. Only when we have tried and failed times without number, when we have reached the end of our resources and the end of our hope—only then are we ready for the miracle of the life of faith. Only then will we experience what has eluded us for so long—the peace and joy and victory that come with trusting Christ for both the pardon and the power.

Why have we been so slow to let God work His wonders in us? We have struggled along with our little five-watt power when we could have been connected with the power that made the worlds! We have taken the slow train when God's planes were flying. We have pushed our trolley cars when power lines were within our reach. As if God had a power shortage and we had to help Him out!

Somehow we can't seem to get rid of the notion that some way we can save ourselves, that we can buy our salvation with our good deeds, that if we just pray hard enough and long enough we can earn our forgiveness.

But think it through. What if heaven had contracted to pay Jesus for His mission to this earth? How much a year? How much a week? How much an hour? Maybe triple time for Gethsemane?

Isn't it an insult to divinity to think that Jesus could ever be *paid* for what He went through? Isn't it an insult to the Saviour to think that we could ever *earn* eternal life by working—or *buy* our forgiveness by the length or detail of our confession? Could all the prayers ever prayed be enough to *pay* Jesus for giving His life? But that's what it cost—His own lifeblood!

No wonder we need to understand our weakness before we are ready for His strength!

Red Stairs to the Sun

Let me take you on another trip today. And I promise you, we will understand "Red Stairs to the Sun" better as a result. In fact, some very surprising and thought-provoking truth will come out of these next few pages. So, I say, let me take you to Petra! The rose-red city half as old as time, carved out of solid rock! For out of this mountain fortress rise the red stairs—red stairs dedicated to the sun!

These are stairs carved by generations long forgotten. These are stairs that led to the high altars of sun worship. Stairs that for centuries felt the endless tread of fascinated, compromising feet climbing to worship a strange, forbidden god.

Red stairs rising from the city of the dead. Silent, crimson symbol of the worship of the sun!

Can you imagine our thoughts—our excitement—as we left the Jordanian desert, approached a precipitous mountain range, and then entered the Siq?

Those straight, towering walls were so close it seemed we could almost reach out and touch them—both of them—at times. Far above us was a narrow strip of blue that told us the sky was still there. And we knew that just a little way ahead—at the other end of the Siq—was Petra, the rose-red city half as old as time!

No wonder Petra was practically an impregnable fortress. For there was no other entrance to the city. Any invading army would have to pass through the Siq virtually single file—and risk a hail of rocks from the defenders above.

It took us thirty minutes to go through the Siq. And then, bursting into view was the ancient, magnificent treasury building, a masterpiece carved out of solid rock. And then the amphitheater, the palaces, the temples, the tombs, the dining halls, the homes. We surveyed them all on horseback, camelback, and jeep, and marveled at these wonders of a past civilization. But we were looking for the red stairs. They were what we had come to see.

Yes, out of this unique and fabulous city of the dead, rise the red stairs that once led to the high altars of sun worship. And as I stood atop those red sandstone steps, it seemed that I could feel the very heartbeat of the great controversy of the ages.

Why? Because here was an ancient center of sun worship—the forbidden worship that for centuries challenged the true God. Here was the altar. And beside it the virgin pool, in which young women were bathed before being burned upon the altar as human sacrifices to the sun!

It is not difficult to understand why a worship like that of Petra—the worship of the sun instead of the God who made the sun—should call for a divine rebuke of some kind. You would expect God to act, to respond to this challenge. Here was a civilization that actually burned its children to its gods. You couldn't expect God to remain silent. Especially when His own people became involved!

You see, in the days of the prophet Elijah, sun worship had filtered across the borders of Israel. The most degrading cults had infiltrated the chosen nation. King Ahab had married Jezebel—a name ever since associated with all that is licentious and vile. The people followed their weak leaders! And what happened? Well, the Bible record tells us what happened.

"So they left all the commandments of the Lord their God, made for themselves a molded image and two calves, made a wooden image and worshiped all host of heaven, and served Baal." 2 Kings 17:16, NKJV.

Here's a very important point. Not only did they turn to the worship of Baal, the sun god. But the worship of Baal also involved turning away from the commandments of God. It's always that way. False worship is not something extracurricular on the side, in addition to true worship. It's a choice. It's one or the other. The difference between true and false worship, then as now, was a difference in attitude toward the commandments of God. There's a clue, friend, if you want to tell them apart.

Imagine how God must have felt. Here was a world He had created—a race lured into revolt by His enemy—a nation for whom He would one day give His life. And now His own people had gone tramping, tramping after other gods!

And so, in the days of Elijah, we see the most dramatic confrontation of all time between sun worship and the worship of the true God. The most dramatic up to then, that is.

It was about 900 B.C. Elijah emerged from seclusion and appeared before King Ahab, demanding that the prophets of Baal, the sun god, meet him atop Mount Carmel. There was to be a showdown. It was to be determined, once for all, who was the true God.

And so they climbed Mount Carmel—450 prophets of Baal, one lone prophet of God, and a multitude to watch the outcome. An altar was built by the prophets of Baal, and all day they begged that heathen deity to send fire to consume their sacrifice. But nothing happened.

And then you remember that Elijah repaired the altar of the Lord, placed a sacrifice upon it, covered the sacrifice and the altar with twelve barrels of water, and prayed a simple, heartfelt prayer. And God heard. Immediately fire descended and consumed not only the sacrifice, but the altar and the stones and the water as well. For He who made the atom knows how to control it!

There, on Mount Carmel, standing alone before the high prophets of Baal and a rebellious people, Elijah called for a choice: "Elijah came to all the people, and said, 'How long will you falter between two opinions? If the Lord is God, follow Him; but if Baal, then follow him." 1 Kings 18:21, NKJV.

How long will you falter between two opinions? The New English Bible says, "How long will you sit on the fence?" It was a call for decision. It was a call to choose between the worship of the true God and the worship of the sun god.

But you ask, What does all this have to do with me? Something very, very interesting, to be sure. Did you know that the Scriptures tell us that Elijah would return—would come back again to this earth? And in our day, at that. Let's read it. It's a fascinating prophecy, right at the close of the Old Testament:

"Behold, I will send you Elijah the prophet before the coming of the great and dreadful day of the Lord. And he will turn the hearts of the fathers to the children, and the hearts of the children to their fathers, lest I come and strike the earth with a curse." Malachi 4:5, 6, NKJV.

The great and dreadful day of the Lord. Well, that's the day just ahead of us. And God is going to send Elijah back in our time.

What do we have here? Reincarnation? Does this mean that we can expect to see the prophet Elijah himself, with his long flowing robes, standing in Times Square in New York City or walking up and down Washington's Pennsylvania Avenue or Market Street in San Francisco? Or Montreal or Sydney or London? I think not.

Actually, this is a prophecy, like many others, that was to have a double application. It was to be fulfilled twice. Elijah would return down here in our time, before the *second* coming of our Lord. But he was also, first, to come into the picture before the *first* coming of Jesus to this earth.

Interestingly enough, the disciples of Jesus were perplexed about this prophecy. They understood it to mean that Elijah would appear before the Messiah. And when they became convinced that Jesus was the Messiah, they wondered why they had seen nothing of Elijah.

So they asked Jesus about it one day, and He told them that Elijah had already come, and they hadn't recognized him. It was clear that He was referring to John the Baptist. But when they asked John if he was Elijah, he said he was not.

Are you a little confused? Well, it all clears up when we read one scripture. It is the announcement of the angel to Zacharias, the father of John the Baptist—before John was born. Listen to what the angel said: "He will also go before Him in the spirit and power of Elijah, 'to turn the hearts of the fathers to the children,' and the disobedient to the wisdom of the just, to make ready a people prepared for the Lord." Luke 1:17.

There you have it. Some of the exact words of the ancient prophecy are quoted. And John the Baptist, the angel said, was to fulfill it.

But no reincarnation, you see. Elijah himself was not to reappear. John was to give a message, he was to do a work, in the *spirit and power* of Elijah. It was the message, not the man, that would reappear.

But was the work of John the Baptist really similar to that of Elijah? Yes, John, from his youth, lived the life of a prophet. In his manner and in his dress he even resembled Elijah. He wore the attire of the ancient prophets—a garment of camel's hair, with a leather girdle.

But that was not the important thing. He spoke in the same spirit and with the same power. He was fearless in denouncing hypocrisy. His message, like that of Elijah, was a call to repent, to reform. It was a call back to the commandments of God. It was a call to decide. A call to choose.

But was John's work in any sense a confrontation with sun worship? Elijah's message was. What about John's message? On the surface it would seem that it was not. Yet if we dig a little deeper, some interesting facts appear.

The Roman Empire was then in power, you may remember. Rome ruled the world. The Jewish people were chafing under Roman rule. A Roman ruler sat in the palace in Jerusalem. It was Herod, the Roman ruler, who attempted to destroy Christ soon after He was born. And interestingly enough, Herod by birth was an Edomite. And it was the Edomites who had inhabited the ancient fortress of Petra, with its red stairs to the sun. Sun worship was in his blood.

And, of course, the entire Roman Empire was riddled with sun worship. God's people were not immune from its influence. And John preached to Jews and Gentiles alike.

The Roman empire, I say, was riddled with sun worship. It was in A.D. 321 that the Roman Emperor Constantine actually decreed that Sunday, the pagan holiday since ancient times devoted to the worship of the sun, should be observed as a day of rest by all in his empire. In fact, in his decree, he even called Sunday "the venerable day of the sun."

Well, that was only 321 years after Christ. But sun worship was not dead, even in the days of John the Baptist.

But now, according to the prophecy, the message of Elijah is to be repeated again just before the second coming of Christ. And just as a message given in the spirit and power of Elijah was to prepare the way for Christ's *first* coming—just so a message similar to that of Elijah will prepare the way for the *second* coming of our Lord.

Just like the message of Elijah and of John, it will be a call to repent, to reform. It will call men back to the commandments of God. It will be a call to decide. A call to choose.

So we ask, Is there such a message today?

Yes, there is. We find it in Revelation 14:6-12: "I saw another angel flying in the midst of heaven, having the everlasting gospel to preach to those who dwell on the earth—to every nation, tribe, tongue, and people." Revelation 14:6, NKJV.

Here it is, represented as given by three angels. God's last call to men. Going to all the world. In our day. The everlasting gospel with a special emphasis on the particular issues—life-and-death issues—that concern every one of us. Brief. Urgent. Nothing could be more important in this end time. It's God's last appeal to men!

How do I know? Because the message is followed almost immediately, in verses 14-16, by the second coming of Christ.

But is there any similarity between this message here in Revelation 14 and the message of Elijah? Yes, there is. A striking similarity. In verse 7 it calls men back to the worship of the true God. Verse 12 indicates that it calls men back to the commandments of God. And verses 9-11 call upon men to choose between true and false worship.

Someone is saying, "Pastor Vandeman, surely you're not going to suggest that sun worship is involved. No one worships the sun today. Sun worship is long dead."

I'm not so sure!

Here's the story. Unfortunately, during the early centuries after Christ, things began to change. Compromising segments of the new church permitted pagan influences to creep in, to corrupt and adulterate the pure teachings of Jesus. Compromise took over. Truth was distorted and confused.

Then came the Dark Ages. Copies of the Scriptures were not readily available to the people. And without the safeguard of God's Word, rites and ceremonies crept into the church that would have shocked Peter and Paul.

Let's take some little things first—things that have no moral significance whatever. They aren't a matter of right and wrong. But I want you to see what has happened.

Have you ever wondered what chocolate eggs and bunny rabbits have to do with the resurrection of our Lord?

Well, according to an ancient legend, an egg of tremendous size fell from heaven into the Euphrates River, and some fish nosed it up on the bank. That's where your egg rolling started. Doves came down and settled on it until it hatched out Venus— known in the East as Ishtar, the great virgin-mother, the goddess of love and fertility, also called the "queen of heaven."

Easter eggs. Bunny rabbits. Fertility, you see.

Now listen. Ishtar, it is said, gave birth to a son, Tammuz, without a father. Here in heathen mythology, centuries before Christ, we find a counterfeit of the virgin birth. Imagine!

Certain of the male gods of fertility became sun gods. They all died every year and had to be resurrected to restore the fertility of plants, animals, and man.

Now Tammuz, the legend says, was killed by a wild boar. And the worshipers devotedly mourned for him for a month every year. Did you ever hear of a forty-day fast before a festival of resurrection? Of course you have.

Even in Jerusalem there were those who wept for Tammuz, the Bible says. And they made cakes to the queen of heaven. Did you ever hear of hot cross buns?

Tammuz was supposed to have been resurrected on the birthday of the sun. That was December 25. Did you ever hear of that date? Since Christians didn't know the exact date of Christ's birth, they took the birthday of the sun.

In Babylon, however, the resurrection of their god, in their New Year festival, was celebrated about the time of the spring equinox. Did you ever hear of a resurrection festival on the first day of the week after the first full moon following the spring equinox? We call it Easter.

But that isn't all. Remember the red stairs of Petra? Those people went up to their housetops every day to burn incense to their sun god. And also they worshiped at their high places, such as the one atop the red stairs. Picture it. Those people climbing to the top of those red stairs early in the morning to watch the sun rise and to worship it.

Sound familiar? Tell me. Did you ever hear of Christians going to the highest place in each city to worship at sunrise? Once a year?

Now please don't misunderstand. These holdovers from paganism are nonessentials. There's nothing morally wrong with eating chocolate eggs or hot cross buns or putting bunny rabbits in a basket for the children. Or climbing to the top of a hill to watch the sun rise—so long as you don't worship it. Or giving gifts to each other at Christmas—even if it isn't the exact date of our Saviour's birth. I say again, these are only fringe issues.

But here is the point. If these fringe areas of Christian worship have been so riddled with the trappings of sun worship, no matter how many good activities have surrounded them through the years, how do we know that some major area of our worship, something *that does matter,* has not been tampered with too? That's my question. And the answer is, we don't.

May I repeat what I have just said? If these fringe areas of Christian worship have been so riddled with the trappings of sun worship, no matter how many good activities have surrounded them through the years, how do we know that some major area of our worship, something *that does matter,* has not been tampered with too? That's my question. And the answer is, we don't.

A few moments ago we were talking about God's last call to men, found in Revelation 14. I mention that it asks men to choose between true and false worship. And it makes it very clear that it's a life-and-death choice. Would you be shocked if I were to suggest that a persistent remnant of sun worship is the key point of contention in this final clash between right and wrong? And it isn't chocolate eggs! It isn't a fringe issue!

Yes, here on the very threshold of the great day of the Lord, that penetrating call of Elijah is heard again. You are hearing it now. "How long will you falter between two opinions? If the Lord is God, *follow* Him! But if Baal is God, then follow *him!*"

Will it be God? Or will it be Baal? Will it be red stairs to the sun? Or a blood-red fountain that can cleanse and cure the sinner's guilt?

> There is a fountain filled with blood,
>   Drawn from Immanuel's veins;
> And sinners plunged beneath that flood,
>   Lose all their guilty stains.

This is the moment to decide. You may not fully understand, at this moment, what all the issues are. But you can still decide, right now, that whatever the issues may be, you are going to take your stand on the Lord's side. You can settle that now.

A Day to Remember

May I take you back nearly two thousand years to the humble little village of Nazareth in old Palestine. It is midweek as we make our way down the narrow cobblestone street, past the little shops with their open fronts. We see the workmen plying their trades as we pass one shop after another. There is a leisurely Middle Eastern atmosphere about it all.

And then we come to a shop that is different. The front is neatly whitewashed, and the street has been recently swept. We enter and find a kindly, stalwart man plying the carpenter's trade, and by his side a young assistant—we would guess about eighteen years of age. The young man is planing a piece of wood, making it true, making it straight. He rests a moment and wipes his brow. As He turns, we see that He has the bearing of a prince, of a king. For He is none other than the prince of heaven, King Jesus, come to cast His lot with the toilers and the poor, to live among men and die in their place.

We hurry on. But we come back again, for we are fascinated by the little shop. We come back on Thursday. We come back on Friday. We come back on Saturday. But on Saturday the shop is closed. The tools have been carefully put away. The shavings have been gathered up from the floor. All is quiet.

We notice that the people are all walking toward a conspicuous building in the center of the village. We follow them and find our seats in the rear of a well-filled meetinghouse. We wait a moment. Then imagine our surprise as we see the carpenter's

Son make His way into the pulpit, open the scroll, and begin to read.

Are we imagining all this? No. The Gospel of Luke tells us something about the worship habits of Jesus.

"He came to Nazareth, where He had been brought up. And as His custom was, He went into the synagogue on the Sabbath day, and stood up to read." Luke 4:16, NKJV.

What are we watching here? A man dutifully conforming to the customs of His day—customs acceptable for His generation but not for ours? Or are we watching the divine Example after whose life every Christian desires to pattern his own?

Are we watching a young Jewish carpenter thoughtlessly following the traditions of His time? Or are we watching a Creator resting on the day that He Himself had set aside for man? What is the truth about what He did that day? What happened to introduce confusion? Has someone turned the sign around? Does it make a difference what day a person observes as the Sabbath? Is any day acceptable to God—Friday, Saturday, or Sunday?

Let me tell you a personal experience that taught me a valuable lesson. I was traveling along the turnpike from Detroit, Michigan, to New York City. I was eighteen at the time, and I was traveling down the highway confident that I was heading for New York City. I had passed Toledo. I had passed Cleveland. I was heading for Pittsburgh, and right straight through to Philadelphia and New York. You couldn't have convinced me—you couldn't have possibly convinced me—that I wasn't heading for New York City. I knew where I was going.

Well, do you know what happened? All at once a Greyhound bus, loaded with people and plainly marked New York City, passed me—going in the *opposite* direction!

I shook myself. I said, "Either that bus driver is wrong, or I'm wrong." Suddenly I wasn't so sure. I was confused. And in this case, confusion was a good thing. And do you know what happened? I drove off the highway into a gas station and, just like our children so often do, I asked my question in the way that I'd get the answer I wanted. So pointing ahead I said to the gas station attendant, "Isn't that the way to New York City?" And he said, "Yes, but it's twenty-five thousand miles that way. And there's a lot of water in between. No," he said, "this is the way to New York City." Evidently I had driven out of a restaurant or a gas station the wrong way, without realizing that I had turned back the way I came.

Friend, could it possibly be that somebody has turned the Sabbath sign around—and some of us didn't know it? I ask again, Does it make a difference which day a person observes as the Sabbath? Is any day acceptable to God?

I would like for us to read three scripture texts for the answer:

"I was in the Spirit on the Lord's Day, and I heard behind me a loud voice, as of a trumpet." Revelation 1:10, NKJV.

Now this scripture doesn't tell us a great deal, does it? It is simply a statement of fact. John was in the Spirit—under the Spirit's influence on the Lord's day.

But there is one thing this scripture does say, and it says it very clearly. It tells us the Lord has a day—the Lord's day, you see. Now it doesn't tell us which one of the seven is the Lord's day—only that the Lord has a day. But that is a step in the right direction. We can no longer say it doesn't matter which day we keep just so long as we keep one day in seven. No, the Lord has a day. Now to the second scripture.

"For the Son of Man is Lord even of the Sabbath." Matthew 12:8.

We have already learned the Lord has a day that He calls His own. And following the Bible formula for discovering truth—line upon line, precept upon precept, you remember—we found more in this verse to add to our first one. It says "Christ is Lord of the Sabbath." So it naturally follows that the Sabbath is the Lord's day. In fact, in the book of Isaiah, God calls the Sabbath "my holy day." So the Lord has a day and that day is the Sabbath. But which day of the seven is the Sabbath? Now to our third scripture: You recognize this immediately as part of the Ten Commandments.

"Remember the Sabbath day to keep it holy. Six days you shall labor and do all your work, but *the seventh day is the Sabbath of the Lord your God.*"

There you have it all put together in one single sentence.

"In it you shall do no work: you, nor your son, nor your daughter, nor your manservant, nor your maidservant, nor your cattle, nor your stranger who is within your gates. For in six days the Lord made the heavens and the earth, the sea, and all that in them is, and rested the seventh day. Therefore the Lord blessed the Sabbath day and hallowed it." Exodus 20:8-11, NKJV.

So the Lord has a day. That day is the Sabbath. The seventh day is the Sabbath. And God considered the Sabbath so important that He made it one of the Ten Commandments.

May I tell you about my father? My father, when he passed away, had been a minister for nearly forty years. Before entering the ministry he had been in business the city of Denver. He was a fine Christian, a Methodist leader of lay groups.

One day out on the shipping platform, one of his workmen had some minor accident and he said something a Methodist shouldn't have said. Well, the other workmen gathered around to see if they could help. When they found the accident wasn't too serious they returned to work. But my father, who had joined them, remained for a moment. He said, "I'm so sorry. I am sure that hurt. But we ought to be a little more careful with our language, don't you think? After all, taking God's name in vain is breaking one of God's commandments. The man spoke up quickly, "Oh yes. Thanks for jacking me up. We Christians do get careless. I appreciate your saying what you did." And they prayed together.

My father started back through the passageway to his office, patting himself on the back that he had helped somebody keep one of the commandments. But all at once a voice spoke to him, "But, Vandeman, you're breaking the fourth commandment!" And it broke his heart.

You see, this truth about the Sabbath had come to my father's attention. For some months he had been battling with conflicting loyalties, trying to make up his mind. He knew what the Word of God said. But there were church ties, his family, his friends, his business. And now he had tried to help somebody else keep the commandments, when he himself was breaking one of them.

He hurried back to his office and dropped to his knees and talked to his Lord. Shortly thereafter he sold his business, and, although he had had a good business education, he went off to a Christian college to prepare for the ministry and became a power in the pulpit for many years.

I would like to ask again, when Jesus went into the meeting-house on that Sabbath, was it only a Jewish carpenter mechanically following the traditions of His time? Or was it the Creator resting on the day that He Himself had made?

Surprising as it may seem, did you know that Jesus made the Sabbath? Did you know that He's not only our Saviour, but also our Creator? Let's read it:

"He was in the world, and the world was made through Him, and the world did not know Him." John 1:10, NKJV.

The world was made through Him—the old King James Version says "by him."

But who is this speaking of? In verse one it says, "In the beginning was the Word, and the Word was with God, and the Word was God." And in verse fourteen it says, "And the Word became flesh and dwelt among us, and we beheld His glory, the glory as of the only begotten of the Father, full of grace and truth," NKJV.

Can this refer to anyone but Jesus? In Colossians 1:15, 16 it says, speaking of Jesus, "He is the image of the invisible God, the firstborn over all creation. For by Him all things were created that are in heaven and that are on earth." NKJV.

Could it be that some of us are learning for the first time that Jesus was our Creator too—long before He was born in Bethlehem. You see, God "gave His Son." He must have had a Son with Him through eternity in order to give Him to us. Jesus our Creator! Yes, in fact, let me put it this way. *If there is no creator, then we have no Saviour.*

How can I make such a sweeping statement? Simply because They are one and the same Person. The Christ of Calvary is the Creator of Genesis. To reject one is to reject the other. The Sabbath, therefore, is not a quibbling over days. It is not an irrelevant hangover from a forgotten past. It is the very heartbeat of the gospel.

Jesus had a perfect right to say, "The Son of Man is Lord of the Sabbath"—because He made it!

Does all this surprise you? Have you been conditioned to think that Jesus attached little importance to the Sabbath?

It is true that Jesus himself said little about the Sabbath. There was no reason for discussion. The identity of the day of rest was never questioned. The only controversy arose over *the way* He kept it. He was continually healing the sick during its sacred hours—and shocking the religious leaders of His day in the process. They never dreamed that He who stood before them was the one who had *made* the Sabbath!

Sometimes we can best discover the strength of a leader's convictions by watching his followers. Shall we, then, move down to the close of Christ's ministry, to that tragic passion weekend, and watch His associates as they came up to the sunset hour, the beginning of the Sabbath, on that dark Friday?

The beginning of the Sabbath—on Friday?

Yes, in the first chapter of Genesis, which contains the account of Creation week, we read that the "evening and the morning were the first day" "the evening and the morning were the second day" "the evening and the morning were the third day." And so on. The dark part of the day came before the light part of the day. So the day, in God's reckoning, begins at sunset. And that means that the Sabbath extends from Friday at sunset to Saturday at sunset. In fact, the Word of God says, "From evening to evening you shall celebrate your sabbath." Leviticus 23:32, NKJV.

Watch His followers then. Jesus has been crucified. Now He has been laid in the tomb. And the Sabbath is approaching. What will they do now? They may have been careful about the Sabbath in the past, but what will they do now—in the hour of the world's greatest emergency? Their hopes had been bitterly blasted that day. They thought they had made a mistake. No words can describe the depths of their despondency, and I need not tell you that despondent people are often careless people. If ever they were tempted to let down the bars, it would be now. And if ever they were tempted to rationalize, it was now.

Yes, if there was anything in the example of Jesus to encourage carelessness about the observance of the Sabbath, anything that would lead them to rationalize around its claims just this once, we shall surely detect it now in the attitude of His closest friends. But let's look at what happened.

"This man went to Pilate and asked for the body of Jesus. Then he took it down, wrapped it in linen, and laid it in a tomb that was hewn out of the rock, where no one had ever lain before. That day was the Preparation, and the Sabbath drew near. And the women who had come with Him from Galilee followed after, and they observed the tomb and how His body was laid. Then they returned and prepared spices and fragrant oils. And they rested on the Sabbath according to the commandment. Now on the first day of the week, very early in the morning, they, and certain other women with them, came to the tomb bringing the spices which they had prepared." Luke 23:52 to 24:1.

We can only conclude that the carefulness of His followers reflects the carefulness of their Lord. If Jesus had any reservation about the importance of the Sabbath, He had utterly failed to communicate it to those who knew Him best.

At this point you may be saying, "How can we *know* which *is* the seventh day—the day that Jesus and His followers observed?"

I once asked that question of an audience. And I must have stopped to catch my breath or something. I had just asked, "How can we know that the Saturday of today is the seventh day of Christ's time?" And just as I paused, someone in the heart of the audience exclaimed so that all could hear, "That's what I want to know!"

You may be surprised to realize that the verses of scripture we have just read make the identification of the day of rest crystal clear. For notice that three consecutive days are mentioned—the preparation day, the Sabbath of the commandment, and the first day of the week. Two are given sacred titles—"The Preparation," "the Sabbath"—and one is given an ordinary number, "the first day of the week." Or to put it another way—the day of the crucifixion, the day Jesus rested in the tomb, and the day on which He was resurrected.

There is nothing better established among the majority of religious scholars than that Jesus was crucified on the day we now call Friday, and that He was resurrected on the day we now call Sunday. The Sabbath is the day between Friday and Sunday. And of course that is Saturday. Could it be more simple?

But now we come to the big question. Since the Bible is so plain that the seventh day, Saturday, is the Sabbath of the Lord, how is it that the majority of Christians keep the first day of the week? Who changed it?

We shall find in our next lesson that the New Testament gives no hint of a change from the seventh day Sabbath (Saturday) to the first day of the week (Sunday). Therefore we must turn to history to find out how, when, and why the change was made.

Shall we let the dark centuries tell their story?

It came about through an involved combination of circumstances. To begin with it was about A.D. 132-135 that a Jewish revolt took place under Bar Cocheba. As a result of this revolt, the Jews were discredited in the Roman Empire. To avoid the persecution that followed, we find Christians increasingly sensitive toward any identification with the Jews. And since Sabbath-keeping was a practice held in common with the Jews, many Christians tended to minimize its obligations.

But persecution was only one factor. The desire for acceptance and popularity was equally responsible for the carelessness that was soon to result in outright apostasy.

The church was quick to see the advantage of compromise with paganism. And it desired the popularity that would come with an influx of new members from the pagan world. To make their invitation more appealing, why not bring into the church some of the popular pagan customs? Would not such a merging of customs cause pagans to feel at home in the church? Why not bring in the pagan day of revelry? Would not the pagans follow their holiday into Christianity?

So began the gradual erosion of the purity of the church—an erosion that spread over several centuries.

It was in the early part of the fourth century that Constantine, the Roman Emperor, while still a pagan, decreed that government offices, courts, and the shops of the artisans should be closed on the first day of the week—"the venerable day of the sun." And it was in the same century that the Council of Laodicea expressed a preference for Sunday.

Since many of the Christians had been sun worshipers before their conversion to Christianity, and sun worshipers had honored the first day of the week for centuries, making Sunday a Christian custom was to the church's advantage—they thought. The church would have more appeal if it accepted some of the pagan customs—they reasoned.

Sunday was brought in at first not as a day of worship, though a worship service was held on it, but as a social day—actually a holiday with a little worship added. For several centuries both days were observed side by side—Saturday as the Sabbath, Sunday as a social day. In fact, this side-by-side practice continued into the sixth century, with the true Sabbath still holding firm in many areas of the Christian world. But as paganism filtered into the church, under the influence of both popularity and persecution, Sunday was emphasized more and more, the Sabbath less and less.

The writings of the early church fathers tell us the story. They traced the progress of the apostasy. They recorded the practices of the early church. Significantly, and please notice this, no ecclesiastical writer of the first three centuries attributed the origin of Sunday observance to either Christ or the apostles. August Neander, a leading historian of the Christian era, writes:

"The festival of Sunday, like all other festivals, was always only a human ordinance, and it was far from the intentions of the apostles to establish a divine command in this respect; far from them and from the early apostolic church, to transfer the laws of the Sabbath to Sunday."—*The History of the Christian Religion and Church,* translated by Henry John Rose, page 186.

And Dean Stanley, in his book *Lectures on the Eastern Church,* Lecture 6, page 291, says, "The retention of the old pagan name 'Dies Solis' or 'Sunday' for the weekly Christian festival, is, in great measure, owing to the union of pagan and Christian sentiment."

In recent years, many knowledgeable Christians who, by the way, observe Sunday themselves have publicly stated or written that the day of worship was changed by man, not God. Here is a statement found in the official Catholic publication *Our Sunday Visitor*, in the issue dated June 11, 1950, a statement upholding Catholic belief in tradition and pointing out the inconsistency of Protestant adherence to it.

The editor of our *Our Sunday Visitor* personally gave me permission to use this statement, and this is what it said: "In all their official books of instruction Protestants claim that their religion is based on the Bible and the Bible only, and they reject Tradition as even a part of their rule of faith. . . . There is no place in the New Testament where it is distinctly stated that Christ changed the day of worship from Saturday to Sunday. Yet, all Protestants, except the Seventh-day Adventists, observe the Sunday. . . . Protestants follow tradition in observing the Sunday."

Has the spirit of the Reformation grown so dim that great bodies of Protestants must turn to the very tradition they reject to find authority for their day of worship? Yet such is the embarrassment of compromise!

Friend, in so serious a matter we must build well. I want you to have the facts. I want you to know them for yourself. Yet how shall I know what to select when the historical references describing this change and the books that contain them would fill a two-ton truck?

Take this, for instance, from J. H. Robinson, in his *Introduction to the History of Western Europe,* page 30. He says, "From simple beginnings the church developed a distinct priesthood and an elaborate service. In this way, Christianity and the higher forms of paganism tended to come nearer and nearer to each other as time went on. In one sense, it is true, they met like armies in mortal conflict, but at the same time they tended to merge into one another like streams which had been following converging courses."

By the way, do you remember our study entitled "Red Stairs

to the Sun"? The Elijah message for the last days warns against sun worship. It makes sense now, doesn't it?

And now listen to this frank statement. William Frederick, in his *Three Prophetic Days,* pages 169, 170, says, "At this time it was necessary for the church to either adopt the Gentiles' day or else have the Gentiles change their day. To change the Gentiles' day would have been an offense and a stumblingblock to them. The church could naturally reach them better by keeping their day."

One shudders to think that such a superficial reason as this should be advanced! But that is what happened. The terrible truth is that the Sabbath of the Lord Jesus Christ was sacrificed to the gods of popularity and compromise!

Cardinal Gibbons said it this way: "You may read the Bible from Genesis to Revelation, and you will not find a single line authorizing the sanctification of Sunday. The Scriptures enforce the religious observance of Saturday, a day which we never sanctify." *The Faith of Our Fathers,* 92nd Edition, page 89.

Sunday—not in the Bible. Not a command of Christ. Only a human institution. True, it came into use early in the history of the church. But is it not a tragedy that it came branded with the name of the sun god, tainted with apostasy, a legacy direct from the bosom of paganism? What a pity that the church received it so willingly, so unquestioningly, so blindly!

How could such a thing have happened? How could such a dramatic fracture of truth have gone undetected? Have we been unwittingly cherishing an institution that is not sacred at all?

Evidently we have. But you see now how it could happen. With nearly twenty centuries intervening since the days of the apostles, many of them dark with the suppression of truth, with the Scriptures available only to kings and the very wealthy, with tradition gradually wedging itself into supremacy in the minds of men—is it any wonder that millions today have never thought to question about the day of rest?

Millions have worshiped on Sunday, considering it a sacred privilege. They have worshiped sincerely, believing it to be the true memorial of our Lord's triumph over death. And God has accepted their sincere devotion. But as the true significance of this matter dawns, what can we do but walk in the light God gives us and let Him make the keeping of the true Sabbath a delight just as He promised to do.

But now shall we turn from the words of men, from the sad story of betrayal, to the words of our Lord. For they are the words of life!

Come with me to the last page of the Bible—to the last page of the book of Revelation, the book written especially for the end time, the book that contains God's last call to men. Listen prayerfully—won't you—as I read from the last chapter of this sacred, saving Book, beginning with verse 12:

" 'Behold, I am coming quickly, and My reward is with Me, to give to every one according to his work. I am the Alpha and the Omega, the Beginning and the End, the First and the Last.'

"Blessed are those who do His commandments, that they may have the right to the tree of life, and may enter through the gates into the city.

"But outside are dogs and sorcerers and sexually immoral and murderers and idolaters, and whoever loves and practices a lie.

" 'I, Jesus, have sent My angel to testify to you these things in the churches. I am the Root and the Offspring of David, the Bright and Morning Star.'

"And the Spirit and the bride say, 'Come!' And let him who hears say, 'Come!' And let him who thirsts come. And whoever desires, let him take the water of life freely.

"For I testify to everyone who hears the words of the prophecy of this book: If anyone adds to these things, God will add to him the plagues that are written in this book; "and if anyone takes away from the words of the book of this prophecy, God shall take away his part from the Book of Life, from the holy city, and from the things which are written in this book.

"He who testifies to these things says, 'Surely I am coming quickly.' Amen. Even so, come, Lord Jesus!

"The grace of our Lord Jesus Christ be with you all. Amen." Revelation 22:12-21.

We have been reading the final words of Scripture. How refreshing they are after digging into the musty records of the past—and hearing about the enemy's attempts to destroy truth. Thank God for these final, positive, encouraging words from our Lord Himself.

I remember so well a pastor friend who had just shared this Sabbath truth with his audience. As the last hymn was being sung he slipped out the side door. He wanted to make his way quickly to the front of the church where he could greet the people as they left.

Evidently a gentleman in the audience that night had slipped out during the closing hymn as well—wanting to be alone, wanting to think and pray.

In the pastor's hurry he almost collided with this tall figure standing thoughtfully in the shadows. He was alone. His eyes were moist. He was deeply moved by what he had heard. The pastor placed a hand on his shoulder, wondering if he could help. The man turned slowly, looked earnestly into the pastor's face, and took hold of his coat lapels as he said, "All my life I have prayed for truth. But I never thought to ask God how much it would cost!"

Yes, truth will cost you something, my friend, and I don't mean money. But it is worth all it costs and infinitely more.

Do you want to thank God for what you have learned from His Word? Do you want to thank Him for the Sabbath and tell Him, cost what it may, you are willing to pay the price and walk in the light He has given you? In the quiet sanctuary of your own heart, you can do this just now.

Since the Day
He Died

Would you turn your thoughts back a few years to a day when suddenly a nation stood still. It was 2:38 P.M., Eastern Standard Time. And it was Black Friday. An hour earlier the first bulletin had interrupted the trivial dilemmas of soap opera characters. Since that moment, news commentators had been moving through the wire releases as gingerly as a buck private through a mine field—afraid of what they would find. And now had come the unqualified word, stripped of all rumor. The President of the United States was dead!

Newscasters tried to control their emotions. People wept openly in the streets as word was passed from mouth to mouth. Shoppers lost heart for their shopping and went home. The stock market slumped and then closed. The eyes of a nation were fastened on the television screen. And for three days and a half they would see not a commercial.

We were stunned. We were bewildered. The deadly aim of an assassin's mail-order rifle had threatened the security of our land.

But then we rallied. To be sure, the law of the land had been seriously broken. The peaceful routine to which we were accustomed had been shattered. But our Constitution, the basic criterion of law and order, remained unchanged. The law had been flagrantly disregarded. But the death of the chief executive had not changed it, or weakened it in the slightest. The three shots fired from that upper room in Dallas, Texas, only tightened our determination that in the future it would be more carefully enforced.

However inadequate the parallel, there was another black Friday. And the heart of the universe stood still!

Men and women were not glued to their television sets the day that Jesus died. Few of them knew or cared what was happening. But Heaven knew. Unfallen worlds knew. Sinless beings watched in stunned silence as they saw their loved Commander dead at the hands of an enemy who had challenged His government.

What they saw that day forever convinced even the wavering among them of the true nature of sin. The character of the fallen angel was finally unveiled. He had gone so far in rebellion as to take the life of the Son of God, his own Creator!

But however jarred, however stunned, however threatened by the enemy's deathblow, heaven rested secure in the knowledge that its government would stand. The justice of its constitution had been eternally vindicated by the death of Jesus. Its law remained undisturbed—except that loyalty to the One who died that day would now make disobedience unthinkable!

Yes, the Son of God was dead. But He had accomplished all that He set out to do. He had made salvation possible for fallen man. But He had done something more. He had vindicated His government. He had, by His own death, shown the unchangeable character of the divine code. He had made the universe secure for eternity. Never again could His law—or His love—be challenged. He had honored the law with His death—and shown the universe how much He cared!

The Son of God was dead. But He would rise again!

Immediately after the death of John F. Kennedy, uncounted memorials sprang up across the land. Jacqueline Kennedy had lighted the eternal flame. Highways, stadiums, and airports were named after him. Cape Canaveral became Cape Kennedy. Lyndon Johnson felt that the most fitting memorial would be to carry out the program interrupted by the Dallas bullet. And so he said, "Let us continue!"

It is only natural that the Christian world should desire to set up a memorial of the death and especially the resurrection of Jesus. Why not, they reasoned—why not make Sunday, the day of the resurrection, a universal reminder of the day He walked out of the tomb and left it empty? It seemed so natural. And so right.

But there is a problem. God Himself has already selected a memorial of His death on the cross. We call it the Lord's Supper—or the communion service.

And every time we share the bread and the wine—the pure, unfermented juice of the grape—it is a memorial of how His body was broken, and His blood shed, for us.

But did you know that God has already selected a memorial of His resurrection? Specifically of His resurrection? And it is beautifully appropriate. Here it is:

"Or do you not know that as many of us as were baptized into Christ Jesus were baptized into His death? Therefore we were buried with Him through baptism into death, that just as Christ was raised from the dead by the glory of the Father, even so we also should walk in newness of life. For if we have been united together in the likeness of His death, certainly we also shall be in the likeness of His resurrection." Romans 6:3-5, NKJV.

Could any memorial be more fitting, more meaningful, than baptism? Immersion represents it perfectly. When a man steps into the water and holds his breath, it symbolizes a death to sin. When he is placed beneath the water, it symbolizes a burial of the old life. When he comes up out of the water, it symbolizes a resurrection to a new life. And by these acts, together, entered into with commitment and with understanding, the follower of Jesus shares in, and commemorates, the death, burial, and resurrection of his Lord. Chosen by God Himself, it is perfect in every detail, incomparable in its parallels. It is difficult to see why mortal man should attempt to improve upon it.

But that is exactly what men have tried to do. For a large segment of the Christian world, asked why it worships on Sunday instead of on the Bible Sabbath, responds that it does it in honor of the resurrection.

But you say, "Memorials are commendable. Couldn't there be more than one in honor of His resurrection?"

Yes, memorials are commendable. But the problem is this: God already has a day of rest. It was established at the end of

Creation week. And it is a memorial too. A very important memorial. Let's read it.

"In six days the Lord made the heavens and the earth, the sea, and all that is in them, and rested the seventh day. Therefore the Lord blessed the Sabbath day and hallowed it." Exodus 20:11, NKJV.

For in six days the Lord made the heavens and the earth. That's why He gave us the Sabbath. It is a memorial of Creation. The Sabbath is a perpetual reminder, every seven days, that we are not the children of chance and accident, but the children of a loving Creator.

Now here is the problem. Are we to have two rest days? One to help us remember His resurrection and one to help us remember that He is the Creator? How would human nature react to having two rest days? Would it not be to choose one or the other? And wouldn't men and women choose the one that is more convenient for them?

This would mean that the resurrection of Jesus is remembered, but His work as Creator is forgotten. God is always honored by our love and devotion, by our remembering the empty tomb. But you see what is wrong here. It is this: The observance of Sunday, sincere though it may be, specifically violates, at least by neglect, one of God's Ten Commandments. For those who observe Sunday are *not* observing the day God has commanded. Can we expect that God will be pleased by a memorial that is tainted with lawbreaking—a loyalty that savors of disloyalty, an offering born of disobedience? Hardly!

Now at this point you may be saying, "I am thoroughly confused. I don't know quite what I have read or where. But I have always assumed that there is New Testament authority for Sunday worship. Have I been dreaming?"

No. You haven't been dreaming. You have simply assumed what millions before you have assumed.

The truth is that the New Testament mentions the first day of the week only eight times. Five of these texts simply refer to the fact of the resurrection being on the first day of the week, which no one questions. They are Matthew 28:1; Mark 16:2, 9; Luke 24:1; and John 20:1. It did happen on the first day of the week. The New Testament tells us so. But is there in these references any intimation—any suggestion—any command to honor that day as a day of rest? Simply reading them will clear up the matter quickly for, as I say, these texts simply refer to the resurrection taking place on that day.

"Now after the Sabbath, as the first day of the week began to dawn, Mary Magdalene and the other Mary came to see the tomb." Matthew 28:1, NKJV.

Notice that the first day of the week begins to dawn *after* the Sabbath. There is certainly no divine direction here asking us to keep the first day of the week as the Sabbath, is there? Now the next one.

"Very early in the morning, on the first day of the week, they came to the tomb when the sun had risen." Mark 16:2, NKJV.

Again simply a factual reference to the time of the resurrection.

And please notice while we are here how verse 1 begins. It says, "Now when the Sabbath was past," the women brought spices so that they could anoint Jesus. Saturday night, you see—after the sun had set. Then early in the morning on the first day of the week they came to the tomb.

The third scripture that mentions the first day of the week is right here on this same page in this same chapter—verse 9.

"Now when He rose early on the first day of the week, He appeared first to Mary Magdalene, out of whom He had cast seven demons." NKJV.

Familiar words. We have read them many times before and again no reference to a Sabbath significance whatever, would you say?

Next we turn to Luke's Gospel.

"Now on the first day of the week, very early in the morning, they, and certain other women with them, came to the tomb bringing the spices which they had prepared." Luke 24:1, NKJV.

Again, it would be helpful to notice the verse immediately before this one—that is, verse 56 of Luke 23. "Then they returned and prepared spices and fragrant oils. And they rested on the Sabbath according to the commandment."

So the women had already rested on the Sabbath before they came on the first day of the week. Again and again we see that the Sabbath comes before the first day of the week—that it is already past when the first day of the week begins. Not much success yet in finding a scripture that authorizes the keeping of the first day of the week as the Sabbath or as the Lord's day.

And keep in mind these scriptures call the Sabbath by its sacred title and the first day of the week by a simple number—"first day."

Now to the Gospel of John.

"On the first day of the week Mary Magdalene came to the tomb early, while it was still dark, and saw that the stone had been taken away from the tomb." John 20:1, NKJV.

There you have it. We have now examined these five scriptures that refer to the fact that Jesus was resurrected on the first day of the week. There's no controversy about these five scriptures whatever.

The next scripture that mentions the first day of the week is in this same twentieth chapter of John, across the page. It is verse 19.

"Then, the same day at evening, being the first day of the week, when the doors were shut where the disciples were assembled, for fear of the Jews, Jesus came and stood in the midst, and said to them, 'Peace be with you.' "

This scripture has sometimes been referred to as a resurrection rally held on the first day of the week by those who seek to find Scripture support for a change of the Sabbath. But it is difficult to see how this could be true since the disciples were gathered behind closed doors for fear of the Jews, and were not yet themselves convinced of the resurrection—until Jesus appeared to them. And, of course, even if it were a resurrection rally, would that make it the Sabbath? Hardly!

Now only two more. The seventh reference to the first day of the week is found in the book of Acts:

"On the first day of the week, when the disciples came together to break bread, Paul, ready to depart the next day, spoke to them and continued his message until midnight." Acts 20:7, NKJV.

Here we read of Paul's preaching a farewell sermon on the

first day of the week, and of the breaking of bread. However, the preaching of a sermon, or the celebration of the communion service, would not make a day the Sabbath. Evangelists often preach every night in the week, and certainly do not consider every day the Sabbath. The disciples preached every day of the week as well. And as for the Lord's Supper, keep in mind that it was originally instituted by our Lord Himself on a Thursday night. But does that make Thursday the Sabbath? I would hardly want to rest my faith on this reference, would you? Especially when scores of references speak of Paul and the other apostles preaching on "the Sabbath." Paul, as his custom was, spoke on the Sabbath. That was his custom. This was a farewell hang-over meeting.

Now we come to the last New Testament reference to the first day of the week. Here it is:

"On the first day of the week let each one of you lay something aside, storing up as he may prosper, that there be no collections when I come." 1 Corinthians 16:2, NKJV.

I think it would be helpful if we were to read the next two verses. "And when I come, whomever you approve by your letters, I will send to bear your gift to Jerusalem. But if it is fitting that I go also, they will go with me." As you read the letters of Paul to the various churches, you will see that he is promoting a project that is very dear to his heart. The believers in Jerusalem are in need of financial assistance. And Paul is asking the churches to put together a large offering for their fellow believers. He seems even to be stimulating a little competition between the churches—to see which can be the more liberal.

This scripture, then—second verse—has nothing to do with going to church on Sunday and putting an offering in the collection plate, as some would have it read. Rather, Paul is simply asking that the Corinthians, when they look over their accounts and see how they have prospered during the past week, put some money aside for this special project, this special offering, so that he won't have to do any fund raising when he comes to visit them. In fact, the various translations of this verse make it clear that this accounting—this "laying aside"—is done at home, not in a worship service. Do you see? The worship service offering is not being described here.

Now there is one more scripture that we should read. It doesn't mention the first day of the week, but many people assume that it does. For that reason we should consider it. We find it in the book of Revelation:

"I was in the Spirit on the Lord's Day, and I heard behind me a loud voice, as of a trumpet." Revelation 1:10, NKJV.

Here it is, some say. John received a revelation from Jesus on the Lord's day—and that's Sunday. But aren't such people assuming too much? First, would receiving a revelation from Jesus make a day the Sabbath? And *is* the Lord's day Sunday? Or are we trying to superimpose one of today's customs upon John and the early Christians? What day *is* the Lord's day— according to what He said through the prophet Isaiah?

"If you turn away your foot from the Sabbath, from doing your pleasure on My holy day, and call the Sabbath a delight, the holy day of the Lord honorable, and shall honor Him, not doing your own ways, nor finding your own pleasure, nor speaking your own words." Isaiah 58:13, NKJV.

God's people had been trampling upon the Sabbath. They had been using it for their own pleasure. And God calls upon them to take their foot off the Sabbath, to turn away from these practices, and call the Sabbath a delight, the holy day of the Lord.

The point is this. As far as the Bible is concerned, God calls the Sabbath "My holy day." Unquestionably, the Sabbath is the Lord's day. And the Sabbath, of course, is the seventh day of the week, not the first.

But before we leave our discussion of Revelation 1:10 and its reference to the Lord's day, I would like you to know something about the origin of the practice of referring to Sunday as the Lord's day. According to the best historical records, the practice of applying that expression to Sunday crept into Christian circles toward the end of the second century. When John wrote this, even those who eventually wanted to see the Sabbath changed had either not been born or at least not even thought of using this expression or of questioning the Sabbath. And the sad fact is that when the expression "the Lord's day" did come into use among Christians, it came tainted with paganism, and specifically with sun worship. Listen to this from Agostinho Paiva, a Portuguese writer on mithraism:

"The first day of each week, Sunday, was consecrated to Mithra since times remote, as several authors affirm. Because the Sun was god, the Lord *par excellence,* Sunday came to be called the Lord's day, as later was done by Christianity."— *O Mitraisimo,* page 3.

Are you shocked at the origin of the practice? "The Lord's day." But the lord referred to was the sun!

Now we must ask, Have we found any Scripture authority for the observance of Sunday? You will agree that we have not. If it is found in the New Testament, it would have been found in these verses we have just read. Read them over again at your leisure, if you would like. The silence of the New Testament concerning any divine change by Christ or the apostles in the day of rest—I say, the silence is deafening!

And this is tremendously significant. For keep in mind that any such change would have excited great controversy among the early Christians. Think of the amount of space Paul gives to the question of circumcision and the relation of Christians to it. He devotes the entire book of Galatians largely to a discussion of the problem. And circumcision had for its authority only the ceremonial law, sometimes called the law of Moses—a law of sacrifices and rites and ceremonies that came to an end when Jesus, the true Sacrifice, the Lamb of God, gave His life. Circumcision is not even mentioned in the Ten Commandments.

Imagine, if you can, the uproar it would have caused if any change of the Sabbath, one of God's Ten Commandments, had been attempted, suggested, or even hinted! We could expect to find many chapters, probably entire books, concerning the matter. And remember that the New Testament was written from nineteen to sixty-three years after the cross. That's a point to remember when you evaluate each of these scriptures.

Unquestionably widespread confusion exists today about God's day of rest. Millions believe that something happened at the cross to undo the authority of the Sabbath commandment. But are we to believe that the Sabbath was seriously challenged while the fires of the early church were still burning bright—and under the watchful eye of the apostles—without a hint of it appearing in the New Testament? Hardly!

Something has happened. Something has gone wrong. Confusion exists. But is God in any way responsible for the confusion? Did He change the Sabbath?

No. God says, "I am the Lord. I change not."

He says, "I will not alter the thing that is gone out of My mouth."

Did Jesus change it? No. On this the Scriptures are very, very clear.

The apostles didn't change it. They observed it, just as Jesus did.

Evidently Jesus did not anticipate or foresee any change in the Sabbath. For in speaking of the destruction of Jerusalem, which would be in A.D. 70, thirty some years later, He told His followers to pray that their flight might not be on the Sabbath.

And what about our day? God's people in this end time are described in the book of Revelation as keeping the commandments of God and the faith of Jesus—and holding to the testimony of Jesus. And in God's last appeal to this generation, found in Revelation 14, He calls upon men and women to worship Him who made heaven and earth. And how better can we worship our Lord as Creator than by remembering, week by week, the day that is a memorial of Creation?

Yes, in all the Scriptures the Sabbath stands secure, enduring, immovable. A memorial of Creation. A specific day, a specific command in the heart of the divine law. A day observed by Jesus and His followers. A day still to be observed in the dark days of A.D. 70. And down in our generation, the Lord's people are designated as keeping the commandments of God and having the faith of Jesus. And notice the urgency in the call to "worship Him that made."

Will the true Sabbath be kept by God's people in the final days of earth's history? It most certainly will.

Have you ever heard anyone say that the Sabbath is a point of controversy? It is. It is a point of controversy because this generation would rather believe in the chance and chaos of billions of years than in the six days of Creation presided over by our loving God. The Lord has a controversy with those who dispute His creatorship. And that's why the Sabbath becomes so important.

Will one day in seven do? As we stand so near the cross, its true meaning dawning more and more upon our minds, how can we even ask? We see that to tamper with the Sabbath would be to tamper with Creation, with Sinai, with Calvary itself. How can we see the Lord Jesus dying on the cross because the law could not be compromised even to save His own life—how can we stand in the blazing light of Calvary and say that this side of the cross it doesn't matter?

Millions were watching television at the moment of confusion when a newsman shouted from Dallas, "He's been shot! He's been shot! Oswald's been shot!" The assassin never lived to face trial or to tell his warped story.

But Calvary's assassin is still at large, and furious because he must soon face a reckoning, furious because his time is short. And don't be deceived. Don't be caught off guard. He is telling a warped story of what happened that tragic weekend. It is his master plot. A plot conceived in the very shadow of the cross!

You see, Satan hated the cross. It was the signal of his doom. It was his sentence of death. He knew it would wrench millions from his control. He dared not fight it openly. But he determined to take it, paint it with his own colors, turn his deceptive floodlights upon it, and place it before the world in a setting that would serve his own evil purpose.

The cross of Calvary had shown the divine law to be unchangeable. But the fallen angel would tell men that the death of Jesus had abolished God's moral code and delivered us from its obligations. He would take the cross which God had used to vindicate the law, and make it a weapon against the law. He would war against the crucified Christ under the pretense of loyalty!

You say it couldn't happen? But it did. It is happening. Millions are deceived.

But against the fallen angel's charges the cross of Calvary stands secure, immovable, and clean. It accepts no responsibility for the widespread disregard of divine law.

What did the assassination of John F. Kennedy do to the Constitution of the United States? Nothing.

What did the death of a President do to the law of the land? Nothing.

What did the death of Jesus do to the divine law? Nothing.

What did the cross do to the Sabbath? Nothing.

Nothing except that the incomparable sacrifice of Calvary, its uncompromising cost to the Son of God, the basic, underlying loyalties it invites from the human breast, make disobedience unthinkable *since the day He died!*

Many years ago I was seated in the dining car on a train. It happened during World War II. I noticed on the back of the menu an engraving of the Stars and Stripes in full color. I've kept it ever since. As a loyal American, I honor the Stars and Stripes. So you can imagine my surprise and my perplexity as beneath the flag I read these words: *"Just as piece of cloth.* That's all it is; just a piece of cloth. You can count the threads in it, and it's not different from any other piece of cloth."

My patriotism would have rebelled if I had not read on: "But then a little breeze comes along, and it stirs and comes to life and flutters and snaps in the wind—all red and white and blue—and then you realize that no other piece of cloth could be just like it. Yes, that flag is just a piece of cloth until we breathe life into it. Until we make it stand for everything we believe in and refuse to live without."

I might take an ordinary piece of red cloth. You could count the threads in it and find it no different from any other piece of red cloth. But if I take the piece of red cloth and a piece of white cloth and a piece of blue cloth and sew them together into the Tricolor of France, Frenchmen would die for it. If I sew them together into the Union Jack, Britishers would die for it. Or if I sew those same pieces together into the Stars and Stripes, Americans would die for it—would not live without it!

Just so, God took an ordinary day. You could count the hours in it. In that respect it was not different from any other day. But then He made a Sabbath out of it. He breathed life into it. He made it stand for everything precious and vital, an emblem of all He wants Christians to live for and refuse to live without.

You see now why the Sabbath is important. If anyone ever tells you that it does not matter, you will understand that it does. Calvary is God's divine testimony to man that those vital words—a part of His eternal law—matter to Him!

The deeper you study into this thing, the more thoroughly you investigate, the greater will be your conviction that something is wrong somewhere, that in some very vital issues we have been just slipping along, following the crowd, never thinking to question.

Yet the example of Jesus is unchanged. There stands the little carpenter shop—closed on Saturday. We shall never find it any other way. It was still the same on that dark Friday, in the shadow of the cross. And it is no different since the day He died!

Centuries Tell
Their Story

I am told that a young Russian czar, many years ago, was walking in the royal gardens one day when he noticed that out in a nearby field a palace guard was standing in all his pomp and ceremony. He asked the young man what he was guarding. The soldier did not know, except that orders called for a sentry at that spot.

The young czar, curious, looked up the records. He discovered that at one time the great Catherine had sponsored acres of rare rose gardens. And on that spot a choice and beautiful rosebush had grown. Every week she permitted the peasants to come and view the roses. But she ordered a sentry to stand guard over that particular bush. The order was never rescinded. The rose gardens had long since disappeared. But a sentry stood guard *over a patch of weeds!*

Could it be that we are earnestly and sincerely standing guard over some things that are not sacred at all? The centuries tell their story.

It is a stabilizing comfort to know that apostasy did not succeed during the lifetime of the apostles, so long as their personal influence was felt by the church. Therefore we shall find no record of it in the Book. But apostasy would not be long in coming. Said Paul, "The mystery of iniquity doth already work." 2 Thessalonians 2:7.

The early church stood forth resplendent in the purity of her teaching, as long as the apostles were among her members. But then came second-generation Christians, a little farther removed from the teaching of Christ and the apostles, a little more susceptible to the perils of popularity and compromise, a little more sensitive to persecution, a little more inclined to fraternize with the pagan world. And it was not long before apostasy wedged into the church—in the form of rites and ceremonies of which Paul or Peter never heard.

Did you know that an ancient prediction places the finger of prophecy on a particular direction that apostasy would take? Listen:

"And he shall speak great words against the Most High, and shall wear out the saints of the Most High, and think to change times and laws: and they shall be given into his hand until a time and times and the dividing of time." Daniel 7:25.

"Think to change times and laws." Evidently we can expect to find a power daring to tamper with the law of God. And that tampering would concern time.

I ask you. What portion of God's law concerns time? Evidently the Sabbath is to be the target of apostasy.

Shall we, then, let the centuries tell their story? And we shall have to turn to history, to early Christian writers. For we shall not find it, I say, in the Book.

It came about through an involved combination of circumstances. To begin with, it was about A.D. 132-135 that a Jewish revolt took place under Bar Cocheba. As a result of this revolt, the Jews were discredited in the Roman Empire. To avoid the persecution that followed, we find Christians increasingly sensitive toward any identification with the Jews. And since Sabbath keeping was a practice held in common with the Jews, many tended to minimize its obligations.

But persecution was only one factor. The desire for acceptance and popularity was equally responsible for the carelessness that was soon to result in outright apostasy.

The church was quick to see the temporal advantage of compromise with paganism. Could they not bring into the church some of the popular pagan customs? Would not such a merging of customs cause pagans to feel at home in the church? Why not bring in the pagan day of revelry? Would not the pagans follow their holiday into Christianity?

The first day of the week had been honored by sun worshipers for centuries. It was on that day that they conducted their most excited demonstrations in honor of the sun. Why not bring Sunday into the church—and pagans with it?

So began the gradual erosion of the purity of the church—an erosion that spread over several centuries.

Now, we are necessarily indebted to the writings of the early church fathers as we trace the progress of the apostasy. These fathers are often quoted in support of Sunday observance. May we just say here that their original writings make very dull reading. Few bother to go to the original sources, but are content to quote them secondhand. Therefore it is often the case that the fathers did not actually say what they are reputed to have said.

However, we must keep in mind that whatever they have said, they have spoken only on their own authority. They were not in any sense inspired. What they have written simply records the *practice* of the early church, not the authority for that practice. Their writings form a part of the record of apostasy. They also indicate that the Sabbath was faithfully observed by many for centuries.

And this is significant. No ecclesiastical writer of the first three centuries attributed the origin of Sunday observance to Christ or the apostles. Listen to this from Augustus Neander, a leading historian of the Christian era:

"The festival of Sunday, like all other festivals, was always only a human ordinance, and it was far from the intentions of the apostles to establish a divine command in this respect; far from them, and from the early apostolic Church, to transfer the laws of the Sabbath to Sunday. Perhaps, at the end of the second century a false application of this kind had begun to take place; for men appear by that time to have considered laboring on Sunday as a sin."—*The History of the Christian Religion and Church*, translated by Henry John Rose, page 186.

It was in the early part of the fourth century that Constantine, the Roman emperor, while still a pagan, decreed that government offices, courts, the shops of the artisans should be closed upon the first day of the week—"the venerable day of the sun." And it was in that same century that the Council of Laodicea expressed a preference for Sunday by stipulating in Canon 29:

"Christians shall not Judaize and be idle on Saturday [Sabbath], but shall work on that day; but the Lord's day they shall especially honor, and, as being Christians, shall, if possible, do no work on that day. If, however, they are found Judaizing, they shall be shut out from Christ."

You notice that Sunday is here referred to as "the Lord's day." Some have thought that John's reference to having a vision on "the Lord's day"—Revelation 1:10—is evidence of the beginnings of Sunday observance in his time. This conclusion is not justified. Evidently he is referring to the Sabbath.

The expression "the Lord's day" was never applied to Sunday by Christians until much later. The first authentic references to Sunday as "the Lord's day" come toward the close of the second century.

Now this slipping away from truth came about gradually. It did not happen overnight, or with a single decree. Sunday was brought in at first not as a day of worship at all, but as a holiday. For several centuries both days were observed side by side—Saturday as the Sabbath, Sunday as a holiday. But as paganism filtered into the church, under the influence of both popularity and persecution, Sunday was emphasized more and more, the Sabbath less and less.

Keep in mind that in those early centuries the Scriptures were not available to every man as now. Doctrines were carried by word of mouth, until the layman could scarcely distinguish between Scripture and tradition. Tradition was more and more accepted as authority. Is it any wonder, then, that such a shocking change in Christian practice could come about through the centuries and become almost universally accepted without being seriously challenged?

There followed the Dark Ages—long centuries when truth was kept from the people. Generation after generation came and went, with few ever knowing the truth as taught by the apostles. The Scriptures were available only to the wealthy, hidden away in musty libraries, or chained to monastery walls.

Then came Martin Luther and the Reformation. Truths long hidden were rediscovered, one by one. Certain backgrounds were laid, certain lines drawn.

You see, tradition had been elevated to a position equal to and even above that of Scripture. So when Luther said, "The Bible and the Bible only is our rule of faith and practice," he threw a bombshell into the thinking of his day.

Perhaps at this point we should define what we mean by *tradition*. By tradition we mean simply the accumulated decrees, actions, policies, and interpretations of the church—its pronouncements touching both theology and moral values.

Then came the Council of Trent. There was no more important council in the history of the church. It convened intermittently for eighteen years, beginning in March, 1545. The question before it was this: Could the *tradition* of the church be successfully defended against the powerful witness of the Reformation, which stood for *the Bible and the Bible only*? It was a question of authority.

For years the question was debated. The council tried to find a logical argument for condemning the Protestant principle of the Bible only as the rule of faith. Many an influential voice exalted tradition above Scripture. "Tradition, not Scripture, Lessing says, is the rock on which the church of Jesus Christ is built."—A. Nampon, *Catholic Doctrine as Defined by the Council of Trent*, page 157.

Yet a strong segment of the council held tenaciously to the view that the church ought to take its stand on the Scriptures alone. And the debate continued. It was a speech by the Archbishop of Reggio that finally turned the tide, that supplied the needed argument in favor of tradition. *He held that tradition must be above Scripture because the church had changed the Sabbath into Sunday on the authority of tradition alone.*

The question was finally settled. But do you see *how* it was settled? Do you see the reason for the position of the council— the reason that carried the day, that finally settled the question for the church as it struggled against the blows of Protestantism's Bible platform? Notice how Dr. H. J. Holtzmann, in his book *Canon and Tradition*, page 263, has summarized the speech that turned the tide:

"Finally at the last opening on the eighteenth of January, 1562, all hesitation was set aside: the Archbishop of Reggio made a speech in which he openly declared that tradition stood above Scripture. *The authority of the Church could therefore not be bound to the authority of the Scriptures, because the Church had changed . . . the Sabbath into Sunday, not by the command of Christ, but by its own authority.*" (Italics supplied.)

What carried the day when all hung in the balance? It was the fact that the church had torn from the law of God one of its precepts—on the authority of tradition!

Are we discovering what happened to the Sabbath? Evidently. Listen to this from the Augsburg Confession, written in 1530:

"They [the Catholic church of the Middle Ages] allege the change of the Sabbath into the Lord's Day, contrary, as it seemeth, to the Decalogue; and they have no example more in their mouths than the change of the Sabbath. They will needs have the Church's power to be very great, because it hath dispensed with a precept of the Decalogue."—Philip Schaff, *The Creeds of Christendom,* Vol. 3, p. 64.

Friend, in so serious a matter we must build well. I want you to have the facts. I want you to read them for yourself. Yet how shall I know what to select when the historical references describing this change would fill a two-ton truck?

Take this, for instance, from J. H. Robinson, in his *Introduction to the History of Western Europe,* page 30: "From simple beginnings the church developed a distinct priesthood and an elaborate service. In this way, Christianity and the higher forms of paganism tended to come nearer and nearer to each other as time went on. In one sense, it is true, they met like armies in mortal conflict, but at the same time they tended to merge into one another like streams which had been following converging courses."

And no less than Dean Stanley, in his book *Lectures on the Eastern Church,* Lecture 6, page 291, says, "The retention of the old Pagan name 'Dies Solis' or 'Sunday' for the weekly Christian festival, is, in great measure, owing to the union of pagan and Christian sentiment, with which the first day of the week was recommended by Constantine to his subjects, pagan and Christian alike, as the 'venerable day of the sun.' . . . It was his mode of harmonizing the discordant religions of the empire under one common institution."

Now listen to this frank statement. William Frederick, in his *Three Prophetic Days*, pages 169, 170, says, "At this time it was necessary for the church to either adopt the Gentiles' day or else have the Gentiles change their day. To change the Gentiles' day would have been an offense and a stumbling block to them. The church could naturally reach them better by keeping their day."

One shudders to think that such a superficial reason as this should be advanced! But that is what happened. The terrible truth is that the Sabbath of the Lord Jesus Christ was sacrificed to the gods of popularity and compromise!

We turn now to the *Catholic Encyclopedia*, Volume 4, page 153: "The [Roman Catholic] Church, on the other hand, after changing the day of rest from the Jewish Sabbath, or seventh day of the week, to the first, made the Third Commandment refer to Sunday as the day to be kept holy as the Lord's Day."

And I read the following statement from the official Catholic publication *Our Sunday Visitor*, in the issue dated June 11, 1950—a statement upholding Catholic belief in tradition and pointing out the inconsistency of Protestant adherence to it: "In all their official books of instruction Protestants claim that their religion is based on the Bible and the Bible only, and they reject Tradition as even a part of their rule of faith. . . .

"There is no place in the New Testament where it is distinctly stated that Christ changed the day of worship from Saturday to Sunday. Yet all Protestants, except the Seventh-day Adventists, observe the Sunday. . . . Protestants follow Tradition in observing the Sunday." (Some smaller Protestant bodies other than the Seventh-day Adventists observe the Sabbath.)

Has the spirit of the Reformation grown so dim that great bodies of Protestants must turn to the very tradition they reject to find authority for their day of worship? Yet such is the embarrassment of compromise.

Amos Binney, a Methodist, writing in his *Theological Compendium*, pages 180, 181, says, "It is true there is no positive command for infant baptism." Then he continues, "Nor is there any for keeping holy the first day of the week."

We could read many such statements. Cardinal Gibbons said it this way: "You may read the Bible from Genesis to Revelation, and you will not find a single line authorizing the sanctification of Sunday. The Scriptures enforce the religious observance of Saturday, a day which we never sanctify."—*The Faith of Our Fathers*, 92d ed., p. 89.

Sunday—not in the Bible. Not a command of Christ. Only a human institution. True, it came into use early in the history of the church. But is it not a tragedy that it came branded with the name of the sun god, tainted with apostasy, a legacy direct from the bosom of paganism? What a pity that the church received it so willingly, so unquestioningly, so blindly!

Have we been caught sleeping? How could such a thing have happened? How could such a dramatic fracture of truth have gone undetected? Have we been unwittingly standing guard over an institution not sacred at all?

Evidently. But I think you can see how it could happen. With nearly twenty centuries intervening since the days of the apostles, many of them dark with the suppression of truth, with tradition gradually wedging itself into supremacy in the minds of men—is it any wonder that millions today have never thought to question about the day of rest?

It could happen. It has happened. We have been standing guard over tradition instead of truth. We are stunned as we see our mistake.

I know that millions have worshiped on Sunday, considering it a sacred privilege. They have worshiped sincerely, believing it to be the true memorial of our Lord's triumph over death. God has accepted their sincere devotion. But now, as the true significance of this matter dawns, as they sense the plot and intrigue involved in this tampering with divine law, they stop short in serious reflection. Disobedience is unthinkable, now that truth has lighted the conscience.

Do you see the new significance now in the question Jesus

asked? "Why do ye also transgress the commandment of God by your tradition?" And He said, "In vain they do worship Me, teaching for doctrines the commandments of men." Matthew 15:3, 9.

The centuries tell their story. The last chapter finds millions standing guard over that which is not sacred at all, holding feverishly to that which is not found in the Word of God.

But there is another side to the story. Truth has not been unattended through the centuries. There has always been a faithful nucleus. Even through the Dark Ages there were those who loyally carried the torch of truth.

Then in the days of the Reformation one truth after another was uncovered and polished bright. One Reformer after another contributed to the growing light and gathered followers about him as he marched forward. Unfortunately, there was a tendency for these followers to stop wherever their leader stopped in the search for truth. They did not continue on in the light of investigation. *And so we have our denominations.* Is it not a paradox that the very struggle to keep truth alive should result in the divisions of Christianity that we know today? Yes, standing guard over what our forefathers taught, rarely thinking to question why. Oh, friend, I determined long ago to find a people willing to stand guard over truth though the heavens fall!

Evidently there is such a group. For John describes a people in these last days who will "keep the commandments of God, and the faith of Jesus." Revelation 14:12.

The blaze of the Reformation that began centuries ago has not entirely dimmed. Its brightest days are still ahead. It will burst into a blaze of glory in these final days of earth's history. I want to have a part in it. "The path of the just is as the shining light, that shineth more and more unto the perfect day." Proverbs 4:18.

Yes, the centuries yield a sad narrative of compromise and plot and intrigue. They also tell a story of faithfulness unto death. There is no more inspiring chapter in it all than the history of the Waldenses.

There in the Piedmont valleys of northern Italy they steadfastly resisted the compromise of truth. They found a haven in those valleys below the Alpine heights, and literally worshiped God in the caves of the earth. There is a great cave over there—you can climb down into it on your hands and knees—where scores of them gave their lives, singing praise to God with their last breath, when they were caught as their enemies built a fire at the opening of the cave.

From childhood they were taught to be missionaries. They copied the Scriptures by hand. Their young men went out disguised as merchants, the precious manuscripts hidden in their clothing, and spread the truth everywhere. Sometimes they paid with their lives.

But there is a tragic sequel to that story. It has haunted me ever since I first heard of it.

It was not long ago that a friend of mine took a group of young people into one of those Piedmont valleys. One evening they were singing around their campfire, telling mission stories. And some of the Waldensian people drifted in and stood listening there in the darkness. Their hearts were touched as they heard young people singing about the second coming of Jesus and preparing to be missionaries as for centuries *they* had been.

When the songs and the stories were over, a Waldensian elder stepped into the light of the campfire and said to my friend, "You must carry on!" And he continued, "We, the Waldensian people, have a great heritage behind us. We are proud of the history of our people as they have fought to preserve the light of truth high upon these mountainsides and up and down these valleys. . . . This is our great heritage of the past, but we really do not have any future. We have given up the teachings in which we once believed."

He pointed to a nearby mountain and spoke of the Waldensian chapels. And he went on, "During the last years in these valleys so filled with sacred history, we have no longer the vision we once had. We have tried vainly to hold our young people in the church. Beside these chapels where it is written, 'The light shineth in darkness,' we have built dance halls, thinking that in this way we might be able to hold our young people. But now they seem to have no more interest in, or love for, the church. Their interest now is down in the bright lights of the big cities. No longer do they want to remain here. What a miracle it is that your church still has young people who are interested in coming up here to our valley to study the history we love so much. But that is all in the past now. The sad thing is that we are not moving forward with courage for the future. *You must carry on!*"

Yes, the words haunt me. They are a sad postscript. Standing guard over truth for centuries—and then losing out. It makes solemn thinking to realize that the children of those whom corruption and persecution and martyrdom itself could not bring to surrender should at last succumb to a life of ease until they could build dance halls beside their chapels and lose their vision, their children, and their hope. It is a sober thought that after centuries of unswerving devotion one of their own number should have to say of their own sacred history, "But that is all in the past now. The sad thing is that we are not moving forward with courage for the future. *You must carry on!*"

Such is the haunting appeal of the Waldenses. Someone must carry on. Someone must pick up the torch of truth laid down by a long-faithful people—*and stand guard till He comes!*

When No Man Can Buy or Sell

For centuries the tyrannical hands of despotic systems had raged in the Old World. We call those days the Dark Ages. A strange colossus—a combination of power both civil and religious—had forged its chains about the minds and souls of men.

The experience of those centuries has taught us that whenever religion reaches out for the arm of the state to enforce its dogmas, the rights of man are buried in the dust. The record is open for all to read.

But oppressed peoples will not always remain oppressed. Persecution spread over Europe to the British Isles. Finally a band of heroic men and women fled to Holland, seeking a place where they could worship God. And then one day they knelt with their pastor on the shore of an obscure Dutch port, and set out, a hundred-odd, first to Southampton, then to Plymouth, England, and finally to brave the Atlantic in the *Mayflower*. Pilgrims, we call them.

Three centuries and more have passed since those first Pilgrims crossed the Atlantic in a cramped, crowded, cranky ship to write liberty across the skies for all the world to read.

But has human freedom ever been in greater peril than today? Freedom, in spite of its proud heritage, can easily be sacrificed upon a careless modern altar. For even as you sit in the comfort and apparent security of your modern home, the enemies of freedom are devising handcuffs for the mind!

May I speak frankly? God, who gave you life, gave you liberty. Your soul is free. No ruler can grant you religious freedom. You have it. That privilege to choose is a gift from your Creator. Rulers can only recognize it.

In fact, the right to think, to think for oneself, is a function of human beings no more to be permitted or denied than the right to breathe. Yet history's most savage tyranny—coercion, imprisonment, torture—has resulted from the desire of the majority to impose their opinions upon the minds of others.

Unfortunately, many who sought a haven of political and religious freedom on the rockbound coast of New England did not extend the same right to others—at least not at first. Those early days were marked with much of the intolerance from which the Pilgrims had fled.

It was James Madison who as a lad heard a fearless Baptist minister preaching from the window of a prison cell, down in old Virginia. From that day there was implanted in him a burning desire to protect for his nation freedom of conscience, if ever his should be the opportunity. Tirelessly he worked, along with others who had the same determination, until the first Amendment was placed to the Federal Constitution. It reads simply and majestically:

"Congress shall make no law respecting an establishment of religion, or prohibiting the free exercise thereof; or abridging the freedom of speech or of the press; or the right of the people peaceably to assemble and to petition the Government for a redress of grievances."

Freedom of religion, freedom of speech, freedom of the press, freedom of assembly, freedom of petition and protest—these were the guarantees.

In the matter of religion those Founding Fathers kept before them one guiding principle—that conscience never belonged to Caesar. Conscience belongs to God. No one ever put it more clearly than Jesus Himself, in Matthew 22:21: "Render therefore unto Caesar the things which are Caesar's; and unto God the things that are God's."

That is what Jesus said. But men have not always done it. Too many Caesars have attempted to force the conscience. Too many groups, large and powerful, have attempted to suppress what they felt was wrong thinking. And too many self-appointed guardians of correct opinion have believed that they could prevent free thinking by persecution.

Now, to be sure, the expression of thought can be prevented by force. Obviously, standing a man up before a firing squad will put an end to his thinking!

But America was not so founded. Free people do change their opinions. But free minds are changed not by force but by the weight of the evidence presented. Chains or bars or flames may alter the outward conduct of a man, if he is weak. But they cannot change his convictions.

Convictions we must have. And a man ought to be ready to defend them with honest, open-minded argument in word and deed. Do not ever succumb to the lukewarm attitude that one position is as good as another. Have your convictions. Live for them. Die for them if necessary. But never forget that your neighbor's convictions are as sacred as your own.

I am thoroughly convinced, for example, that the earth is round, that the democratic form of government is superior, that the family is a sacred unit ordained by God, that true religion is indispensable, and that Christ is the Saviour of men. But I have not the slightest desire to torture, imprison, or defame the man who differs with me.

The right to differ, whether a man is right or wrong, is a sacred legacy that must be defended at all costs. Unfortunately, sometimes the most intelligent defenders of political liberty are the first to be guilty of bigotry, to put chains on religious freedom.

Such is the intolerance that has painted crimson the pages of history. I urge you, never become a party to coercion of the conscience in matters of faith and morals. Why? Let me illustrate.

Suppose that zealous, well-meaning Christians in a free land should campaign until they get a law enforcing baptism. Now baptism is certainly right. It is Scriptural, for our Lord Himself said in Mark 16:16, "He that believeth and is baptized shall be saved."

Suppose, then, that I manage to get hold of a man who is smaller than I. I tell him he is going to be baptized. But he says, "No, I'm not." I say, "Yes, you are. The law says so." He replies,

"I don't even believe in Jesus." But I say, "Never mind. The law says you must be baptized."

You see at once the folly of it all. You see that even things right in themselves become wrong if forced upon the conscience.

Another illustration. Suppose I call across the fence to my neighbor and say to him, "The next time I hear you swearing, I am going to turn you over to the law." There are laws against swearing, you know, even today.

But in the early days the penalties were severe. In my own state of Maryland, in the year 1723, there was a law providing that a man who was caught swearing or speaking blasphemy, cursing God, or denying Christ, would "for the first offense be bored through the tongue and fined twenty pounds sterling." For the third offense the penalty was "death without the benefit of the clergy."—*American State Papers*, page 49.

Nor was it only swearing that was punishable by law in those early days. Before the principles of liberty and freedom were embraced in the Constitution, there were also numerous laws requiring a strict observance of Sunday, the first day of the week. In Virginia, for instance, in 1610, it was required that all attend divine services on Sunday morning. The man who chose to stay at home lost his allowance for the entire week following. He was whipped on the second offense. And for the third offense he was "to suffer death."—*American State Papers*, pages 19, 20.

So you see, our baptism illustration was not so ridiculous after all. These things actually happened. And they can happen again!

I wonder if you realize that you could discover Sunday laws on the statute books of nearly every state today. Some of them are old and inactive, to be sure. But a surprising number of them are new, enacted in recent months and years—*in spite of the Constitution!* In fact, as late as 1963 two hundred forty Sunday bills were introduced into forty-one State legislatures.

And there are deeper issues involved in these laws than appear on the surface. Legislation regarding a day of rest may appear harmless, commendable, humanitarian. But do you see the danger? Do you see what could happen—even in America, even in a free country, even in your hometown?

Many a man sincerely believes and practices the command of our Lord to worship on the seventh day, just as it is enjoined in the fourth commandment. In many a breast the conviction is deepening that loyalty to the crucified Christ demands nothing less than such obedience. But the seventh day, of course, is Saturday. Has any nation, any state, the right to force the keeping of Sunday upon the consciences of men who believe otherwise? Would not such legislation place many a Christian of deep conviction in a circumstance where he must say with the apostle Peter, "We ought to obey God rather than men"? Acts 5:29.

Do you see? The real issue is more than baptism, more than refraining from swearing, more than a day of worship—as important as these are. The real issue is the conscience. The conscience is at stake!

We are a generation tired of bigotry. We have read its awful story on pages crimson with the blood of martyrs. Our nation was founded by those who fled from it. But now the mistakes of past centuries have been acknowledged and repudiated. We want to be through with it.

Even in our own lifetime we have seen too much of it. Hate and bigotry have raised their ugly heads in national elections. Americans elected a Catholic President for the first time—not only because he was a brilliant statesman and keen politician, but because they wanted to show the world that America was through with bigotry. And then we saw our beloved President cut down in his youth by bullets of hate. We wanted no more of it. We determined to purge our national conscience of bigotry and hate, whether of race or creed.

But are we through with bigotry? At the risk of being misunderstood I must share with you the conviction that we are about to witness the worst bigotry the world has ever known. I base that conviction on the clear and unmistakable word of the living God. For uncannily Revelation describes the impasse and defines the issues in this controversy of controversies. Listen!

"And he causeth all, both small and great, rich and poor, free and bond, to receive a mark in their right hand, or in their foreheads: and that no man might buy or sell, save he that had the mark, or the name of the beast, or the number of his name." Revelation 13:16, 17.

Evidently we are not through with bigotry. Here in these last days—I sincerely believe it will be in our lifetime—a mark is to be imposed, some religious obligation is to be made mandatory, under threat of boycott or even death. For verse 15 says: "He had power to . . . cause that as many as would not worship the image of the beast should be killed."

Here is no ordinary boycott. Here is not a national strike. We are not reading about riots in the streets. These things are child's play compared to the issue before us. Evidently the mark, the obligation to be imposed, is something particularly offensive to God, a direct affront to Himself and His government. For notice what He says about it in Revelation 14:9, 10:

"And the third angel followed them, saying with a loud voice, If any man worship the beast and his image, and receive his mark in his forehead, or in his hand, the same shall drink of the wine of the wrath of God, which is poured out without mixture into the cup of His indignation; and he shall be tormented with fire and brimstone in the presence of the holy angels, and in the presence of the Lamb."

Before us is an issue that concerns every man. For the Word of God says, "If any man . . . receive his mark." *If any man*— even with the threat of boycott held over him! *If any man*— whatever his faith or philosophy of life! *If any man* receives the mark, there is in store for him the unmingled wrath of God!

Evidently God feels very deeply about this. This matter must carry with it an urgency equal to or surpassing anything else we might discuss. For regardless of what that mark may be, I think you will agree that we ought to discover what it is so that we may avoid it.

Revelation 13 is a most unusual chapter in this book of last things. Reading it, we are struck with the similarity, especially in verse 5, between the power described here and the one spoken of in Daniel 7:25—the power that would tamper with God's law.

Is this why the anger of God is aroused to speak the most

solemn warning to be found in the Book? Does the issue touch His law? And dare we suggest it? Could the day of rest be involved?

The Geiger counter ticks loudly as we think of the rash of Sunday laws being enacted, and the pressure for more. Are we watching the beginnings of what divine prediction says will come? Could Sunday be involved? How could Sunday be a mark?

Come back again to the Council of Trent. Read again the statement of Dr. Holtzmann:

"Finally, at the last opening on the eighteenth of January, 1562, all hesitation was set aside: The Archbishop of Reggio made a speech in which he openly declared that tradition stood above Scripture. *The authority of the Church could therefore not be bound to the authority of the Scriptures, because the Church had changed . . . the Sabbath into Sunday, not by the command of Christ, but by its own authority."—Canon and Tradition*, page 263.

What carried the day when all hung in the balance? The fact that the church had torn from the law of God one of its precepts. The fact that the day of worship had been changed not by Christ's command but by the authority of the church—*it was this act that was held up by the church as its mark of authority in religious matters!*

That act, friend, is still held up before the world as a mark of ecclesiastical power. Listen to this from *A Doctrinal Catechism*, by Stephen Keenan, an approved work.

"Q. Have you any other way of proving that the church has power to institute festivals of precept?

"A. Had she not such power, she could not have done that in which all modern religionists agree with her;—she could not have substituted the observance of Sunday the first day of the week, for the observance of Saturday the seventh day, a change for which there is no Scriptural authority."—Page 174.

And this from *An Abridgment of the Christian Doctrine*, by Henry Tuberville, D.D., of Douay, France:

"Q. How prove you that the church hath power to command feasts and holy days?

"A. By the very act of changing the Sabbath into *Sunday*, which Protestants allow of; and therefore they fondly contradict themselves, by keeping *Sunday* strictly, and breaking most other feasts commanded by the same church."—Page 58.

This dispensing with one of the precepts of the Decalogue and substituting in its place a day God never commanded, is claimed as the mark of authority to bind the consciences of men. However appalling the revelation, this establishment of the first day of the week as a day of worship in spite of God's clear word that the seventh day is His Sabbath—this, by overwhelming evidence and forthright admission, must be the mark so soon to be imposed!

Do you begin to see what the real issues are in this final conflict? This thing is not done in a corner. It holds the center of the stage in last-day Bible prediction. And yet some thoughtlessly ask, "Does it make any difference?" God will help us to see that it does.

God is bringing this issue to the attention of men at a time when it is soon to be needed. True, the church may be outwardly changing. Its current pronouncements, commendably, are based upon Scripture rather than tradition. But its sweeping reforms have to do with the externals and not with doctrine. They do not repair the serious fracture in the law of God for which the church through the centuries has accepted responsibility.

Nor is the church today any more reluctant to seek the cooperation of the state. And whenever church and state unite to legislate spiritual issues, persecution follows.

Yes, it is to this generation tired of bigotry that God points the most severe test. And you and I will stand only as we discern the true principles involved. For just as the Pilgrims unwittingly became persecutors, so men today who hate bigotry may themselves become a part of a great persecuting flood that will shock men and angels!

Remember the supermarkets? Certain business houses, you see, had contended that since the First Amendment of our Constitution forbids the passing of any law respecting religion, the state laws requiring Sunday closing were therefore unconstitutional. They took their cases to the Supreme Court. I sat in those historic chambers and listened as, to the surprise of many, that highest Court—though three justices dissented— ruled that Sunday-closing laws were not religious anymore, but somewhere along the way had become only social and welfare legislation.

And so, with the encouragement of the Supreme Court, new Sunday-closing laws are being passed. And old ones on the books—some more than a century old—are being dug up and clumsily enforced.

We smile at the strange distinctions between what can be sold on Sunday and what cannot be sold. It is all very confusing. As we scan the various laws, we find an almost unbelievable hodgepodge of bans and exceptions. You can buy a hammer but not nails, a bird but not a cage for it. You can buy beer for yourself, but not milk for your baby. You can purchase an antique, but you dare not acquire a piece of *new* furniture. I ask you, What does such chaos have to do with health and welfare?

No, friend. It is more than supermarkets. It is more than concern for the hours put in by the laboring man. Believe me when I tell you that the entire issue of religious freedom is seriously involved. What we are viewing here is a subtle but deliberate intrusion upon the right of free men. But it has slipped in under a smoke screen of pretended innocence. It has blinded the eyes of thousands who would die for the cause of religious freedom— *if they knew what was at stake.*

Let me illustrate. Suppose that down the street we have a small business operated by a Seventh-day Adventist. One of his employees is a dependable young Mohammedan—a naturalized American. Now the law requires that the business close its doors on Sunday. The Seventh-day Adventist, because he sincerely believes Saturday to be the divinely appointed day of rest, must also close on Saturday. And his Mohammedan employee, whose day of rest is Friday, must lose three days of work each week—or violate his conscience. One or the other!

Suppose, if you will, that political power in our nation were to come into the hands of a few of our Mohammedan friends, who after coming into authority should pass a Friday-closing law.

Would we accept it without protest as simply welfare legislation? Think it through.

And yet thousands of dedicated, loyal Christians, not recognizing the tremendous issues involved, are crusading against Sunday shopping with bumper stickers on their cars. Little do they dream that they who so hate bigotry are being unwittingly drawn into the vortex of the most serious bigotry of all. Little do they dream that the time will soon come when no man can buy or sell unless he has the mark. Little do they dream how short is the trail from crusade to persecution.

The conscience is at stake. And conscience is not the domain of the state. There is something in man that is more than bone and nerve and cell—something more than muscle that tires after a forty-hour week. Conscience is something that belongs to the Creator—something with which both God and our founding fathers have forbidden the state to meddle.

Man is born free—free to think, to choose, to act according to his convictions, whether right or wrong. He is free to die for a good cause—or for a bad one.

Conscience is the sacred inner sanctum into which God Himself will never enter uninvited. It is that sacred inner room in which the soul decides. God impresses. God guides. God has written. But God does not force. He will not go in, nor will He allow anyone else to go in except by the choice of the individual.

Satan would like to force his way in. Sometimes loved ones would like to enter—loved ones who do not understand. Sometimes the power of the church, and sometimes the power of the state, would like to enter. But God Himself guards that door. His flaming sword forbids coercion from friend or foe. The soul is free. Christ made it free—on Calvary!

Yes, it costs something to confess Christ. Unfolding truth often comes as a surprise. And truth can be very disturbing at times. For suddenly we discover that the price is high.

A pastor had just talked with his audience about the day God says to remember. As the last hymn was being sung he slipped out the side door. He wanted to make his way quickly to the front of the auditorium where he could greet the people as they left.

In his hurry he almost collided with a tall, manly figure standing thoughtfully in the shadows. He was alone. His eyes were moist. The pastor placed a hand on his shoulder, wondering if he could help. The man turned slowly, looked earnestly into the pastor's face, and said, "All my life I have prayed for truth. But I never thought to ask God how much it would cost!"

Truth will cost you something. But it is worth it—even if it means to be different.

It was Henry Thoreau, that rugged New England individualist of the nineteenth century, who once commented: "If a man does not keep pace with his companions, perhaps it is because he hears a different drummer. Let him step to the music which he hears, however measured or far away."

Desmond Doss is a man who heard a different Drummer. A medical corpsman in World War II, he is a shy, almost frail-appearing man that you would not suspect of great courage. But he wears the Congressional Medal of Honor.

This is how it happened. It was a Saturday morning on Okinawa. Desmond Doss, because it was the Sabbath, was off duty. But the Army was about to make another attempt to take Hill 167, and no other medical corpsman was available. Would he go with them?

He replied that of course he was willing to save life, even on the Sabbath. Quickly he gathered his equipment. But then he asked them to wait. "We dare not go up that hill without prayer," he said.

And so the United States Army waited, while Desmond Doss prayed aloud. But they were willing to wait. They had confidence in this man, and in his prayers. Somehow they felt a little safer.

They made their way up the steep escarpment, but were soon beaten back by the enemy. And when the roll was called, Desmond Doss was among the missing. But suddenly they were attracted by someone waving from the top of the cliff. There he was, beckoning them to help.

Immediately he was ordered to come down. But orders meant nothing to him when lives were at stake. When they saw that he meant business, they went to his aid. They tossed hand grenades over the cliff to cover him, and he began to work. Single-handed, under enemy fire, one by one he lowered seventy-five men to safety!

Seventy-five men lived—all because of one man who heard a different Drummer—who dared to be different!

On a Friday Night

The life story that I know best began in the shadow of Pikes Peak in beautiful Colorado.

I was born into a minister's home. And there were three other children to welcome me.

I suppose that if I were to tell you all about those early days, all the little intimacies, one moment you would be delighted, another moment there would be a tear in your eye. Another moment I think you would be a little surprised, or even shocked at all that happened.

For my early years, rather than being the cloistered seclusion that so many associate with a minister's home, were actually a realistic exposure to life.

My father, you see, was not simply a preacher. He was a true helper of men and women. And he wisely exposed me to enough of his experiences to make a profound impression on my young mind.

I learned very early that sermons do not come alone from study and discipline and wide reading alone, but from life. I knew even then that I could never choose the gospel ministry lightly.

You see, even during those first years of adolescence, gnawing away at my restless mind were the first faint suggestions that God might someday call me into the gospel ministry. I confess that the idea surprised me. And the truth is that it was to surprise those who knew me even more. In fact, I am a little embarrassed even yet when I meet someone who knew me dur-

179

ing those early years. For I don't know just how much they remember!

Yes, God was calling me even then. But these were convictions that from the beginning I was determined to stifle. I set out to break away from what I foolishly called restriction into what I mistakenly called freedom. I didn't realize how wrong I was.

I tremble to think of what I so narrowly escaped. No. There wasn't any trail of scarlet sin in my life. Nothing to disgrace my family or the church. Nothing revolting to society.

You see, conversion for such individuals is easier. For unless a man has completely blunted the voice of the Spirit he knows where he stands. He recognizes that he is lost. He knows he needs God.

But I was gripped by something worse. Mine were respectable sins. I was lost in the church. Don't let anybody ever tell you that you can't be lost in the church. Because you can!

Please believe me. It is altogether possible to accept a theory, to be satisfied with a form of religion, and yet be lost—lost *in* the church.

Oh, I would go to church and hear a sermon, and I would be concerned. I would read the newspaper and see prophecy fulfilling, and I would be troubled. But when I tackled my own natural weaknesses, I was utterly helpless.

I knew what was right. There was no problem there. But religion, at least my experience with it, seemed to be very weak on the *how*. My promises were like ropes of sand.

I tried whipping up the will. But it didn't work. And then I became rebellious. I tried to get away from it all. I tried to bury myself in a round of activity.

Yes, I became so weary of defeat that I tried to run away from conscience. But thank God, conscience, unless you kill it, unless you kill the watchdog—conscience will never let you go.

I thank God for the voice of the Spirit. I love to talk about the Holy Spirit.

But now for a moment I want to share with you my most serious conflict. It's something that I don't tell easily. But I discovered that people were helped and encouraged by it, for I'm just an ordinary individual, and I've found that whatever helps me, helps others.

But keep in mind that I am not simply telling my story. The real issue is—how are people saved? It's the *how* of salvation that so few people understand. It is this that we are interested in discovering.

During those troubled years I tried to bury myself in a round of activity and entertainment, trying to forget God. I couldn't stand to be alone. I was thoroughly bored.

Finally, I couldn't stand it any longer. It was a Friday evening, and I was seated in a meeting where my father was speaking. I can picture it all so clearly. There he stood, that dear man of God with flowing white hair and a kind, compassionate face. He has always been my ideal of a minister.

Now evidently he was speaking to the entire congregation, not to me in particular. But every word he said cut like a knife. I got up, walked out of that meeting, and moved into the shadows.

I shall never forget those moments. For in that quiet, balmy evening, looking up past the trees into God's great sky, I actually shook my fist at the heavens and said, "Holy Spirit, leave me! And don't ever come back!"

A terrible thing to say! Bitter words! And yet those words were prayer, even though they were bitter in their defiance. And God answered that prayer. He answered it just the opposite of the way I asked it.

Well, that experience was the climax—the climax of a long series of events in which the enemy had been overstepping himself, going too far. I had been doing things that surprised and amazed even myself.

I began to read the fine print on the devil's contract. I saw what was wrong with it. And I decided to break it. But how?

Little did I know that I was standing on the threshold of an experience that would dwarf all my former dreams of personal happiness. I was to learn a secret that would not only save my own restless soul, but would help millions who are secretly longing to know.

For many months that simple secret seemed to evade me. I

set out at once to reconstruct my life. Vigorously I attempted to set my house in order. But I was weak on the *how*.

What worried me then was that no matter how hard I tried, I repeatedly failed. I worked hard enough. I tried hard enough. But hard work evidently wasn't the answer. And I didn't know!

Complicating the problem was this. I noticed that when certain older Christians were asked just how to overcome temptation and the power of wrong habit, the counsel invariably seemed to be "Try harder."

So although it sounded a little too much like self-hypnosis, I whipped up the will again, flexed my muscles, and made another try. But after a while, as my will relaxed, I found myself back where I had started. This produced discouragement, of course. And if there was anything I did not need at the time, it was discouragement.

Try harder. That was the counsel.

Listen. If anyone tells you to try harder, tell them they're wrong for however well meaning the counsel, however necessary it is for us to cooperate with God, simply trying harder isn't the answer. The old Methodist hymn said it so well:

> Not saved are we by trying;
> From self can come little aid;
> 'Tis on the blood relying,
> Once for our ransom paid.
>
> 'Tis looking unto Jesus,
> That Holy One and Just.
> 'Tis His great work that saves us;
> It is not try, but trust.

Try harder? Try until you are weary. Try until you're worn out. But still your weakness will mock you. Frantically trying only focuses attention upon yourself. It is the power of God that saves. The only way to get into the kingdom of heaven is to be born into it. It's just that simple. But I didn't understand.

I knew that something was wrong, desperately wrong. I dropped to my knees to plead with my God. I opened the Word and studied it carefully. For if this business of Christian living was genuine, there would need to be a more adequate demonstration of it in my life.

And now came the surprise. For as I opened the Scriptures I found little emphasis on trying harder. Instead I discovered such words as these.

"Can the Ethiopian change his skin or the leopard its spots? Then may you also do good who are accustomed to do evil." Jeremiah 13:23, NKJV.

And then I saw the same thing clearly described by the Saviour.

"You will know them by their fruits. Do men gather grapes from thornbushes or figs from thistles? Even so, every good tree bears good fruit, but a bad tree bears bad fruit. A good tree cannot bear bad fruit, nor can a bad tree bear good fruit." Matthew 7:16-18, NKJV.

No wonder it could not be done by simply trying! I said, "Lord, thank You. This makes sense." I began to see now why simply trying had proved so futile. Evidently God wanted to do something deep and fundamental within me, and I had not permitted it.

A friend of mine helped me tremendously one day with an illustration about a wolf and a lamb.

Shall we suppose, my friend suggested, that a wild timber wolf should watch and admire the habits of a flock of peaceful sheep and decide that is the way an animal ought to live. Suppose the wolf attempts now to live just as a sheep lives. When the sheep follow the leader, he follows the leader. When they eat grass, he eats grass.

Would not that wolf have a difficult time? Wouldn't he slip back to his old way of life? Of course. He has a wolf nature. Green grass would seem tasteless as he remembered feeding on some dead carcass.

Yet, if one of the sheep should say, "How are you getting along, being a sheep?" the timber wolf might answer, "I'm doing the best I can."

Doing the best I can. Did you ever hear anyone say that? Did you ever say it yourself? Oh friend, God wants to do infinitely more for you and me than the meager results of our own self-generated effort.

But listen. Suppose that God, by a miracle known only to the Creator, should transplant into the wolf the *nature* of a sheep. Then would it be difficult to live like a sheep? Not at all.

I remembered the visit of Nicodemus to Jesus by night, and those unforgettable words, "You must be born again." They made sense now. I began to understand what He meant.

And I understood now the words of Paul that had seemed so hopeless before. It was all beginning to fit together.

"Therefore, if anyone is in Christ, he is a new creation; old things have passed away; behold, all things have become new." 2 Corinthians 5:17, NKJV.

It was in the Book all the time. It was not new because I had discovered it. But as the secret unfolded, as each door opened, I stood in wonder before the utter simplicity of God's plan.

My wonder deepened as it all seemed to fall in place. It was a new nature that I needed. And evidently such a transformation was possible. But how could it be brought about? I was simply helpless. But thank God that I was. For this sense of helplessness opened the door.

It was in the book of John that I found the answer.

"But as many as received Him, to them He gave the right to become children of God, even to those who believe in His name: who were born, not of blood, nor of the will of the flesh, nor of the will of man, but of God." John 1:12, 13, NKJV.

The new birth was not something that could come about through the will of man. No wonder I had failed!

True, I had changed direction. I had decided to break my contract with Satan. I had faced the unpleasant task of confession. I had felt the grief that Peter must have felt when he betrayed and denied his Lord. I had come to the place where I could say sincerely, "I am sorry. No one else is responsible. I am to blame. God help me!"

All this was opening the floodgates, you see, for the new birth. But nothing I could do could bring it about.

Unquestionably I was facing a miracle. And did I have to submit to a miracle? Evidently.

I saw now that the Christian life is not simply a modification or improvement or fixing over of the old. Instead, it is a transformation, the changing of a person's nature, by the power of the Creator. Ever since the day I discovered that secret my greatest happiness has been to see the light in the eyes of men and women as this truth dawns.

It all came about so effortlessly. And I had tried so hard! Listen to these words from what I believe to be an inspired book:

"No one sees the hand that lifts the burden, or beholds the light descend from the courts above. The blessing comes when by faith the soul surrenders itself to God. Then that power which no human eye can see creates a new being in the image of God." *The Desire of Ages*, page 173.

No one sees the hand. But the miracle is there.

Tongue cannot tell it! Pen cannot write it—the peace, the release that full surrender brings to the human breast! This is the transforming secret that was to dwarf every youthful dream I had ever known into insignificance. Not fitful, restless, self-dependent trying. No. Simple trust. I learned it the hard way. But I learned it never to forget!

Let me take you back to that Friday night when I stood in the shadows, looking up at the stars. If I had been examined that night on the theory of truth as it is taught in God's Word, I would have passed with flying colors. In fact, if my father had been called way from his meeting by some emergency, I believe I could have clearly presented his subject. But it was not theory I needed—or clarity. It was life!

I knew then and there that if ever these lips were commissioned to share truth with others, power must attend it or it would accomplish nothing. I knew even that night the terrible responsibility of the ministry. For no man or woman is ever the same after he has heard the claims of Christ upon his soul.

Yes, I knew then, as I know much better now, that it is possible to accept a theory of truth and yet be lost. For without the transformation that comes through divine power, the original tendencies to sin are left in the heart in all their strength, only to forge new chains and impose a slavery that the power of man can never break!

I had so narrowly escaped such a slavery that I determined no one within the hearing of my voice would ever remain unaware of its danger. God help the person who rests passively under the shadow of a superficial profession, an outward cover-up of religion! He is the person I sincerely pray my ministry may help.

I realize now that the struggle of that Friday night under the stars was in reality the beginning of my ministry. God knew that the real desire of my heart was just the opposite of the words that escaped those lips. The deepest cry of the soul—that His Spirit might *never* leave—is the prayer He heard that night. And forever I thank God!

First, You Look

Suppose, if you will, that you are a newspaper reporter in old Jerusalem, about nineteen hundred years ago. Word has just come in that Jesus of Nazareth is in the city, and you want to be first to interview Him.

So you hurriedly scribble some questions on your note pad and set out to find this much-talked-about Teacher.

Let me warn you that you may forget your questions. You may even forget why you are there. This Man Jesus has a way of so capturing attention that people forget everything else.

On one occasion a crowd became so absorbed in His teaching that they listened all day and forgot that they hadn't eaten. It was Jesus who reminded them that they must be hungry.

His enemies once sent officers out to arrest Him. They came back without Him, explaining, "No one ever spoke the way this Man does!"

A Samaritan woman brought her waterpot to the well where Jesus was resting. He told her about living water. She was so fascinated that she forgot her waterpot.

Never have people been so fascinated by any other man. But then that isn't surprising. Because never, before or since, has there been such a Man!

Jesus walked by the Sea of Galilee one day. He saw two men in a boat fishing. He said, "Follow Me." They did. Immediately.

He passed by a tax collector's booth and said to the tax collector, "Follow Me." And the man, without hesitation, left his revenue collecting—and followed.

A woman in need of healing pressed through the crowd, determined to touch the hem of His robe as He passed by. She did. And she was healed.

A man short of stature climbed a tree to get a glimpse of the Teacher as He passed. Jesus looked up and spoke to him. And in that moment Zaccheus became a devoted follower.

Time and again His enemies mingled with the listening crowd, determined to trap Jesus in His talk. Instead, He trapped them.

There was a man named Nicodemus, a man prominent in the religious community. He sought out Jesus at night so as to avoid the criticism of his colleagues. He expected a challenging intellectual exchange. Instead, Jesus told him that what he needed was to be born again. And it took him a long time to figure that out. In fact, he never really understood that memorable night interview until the day he saw Jesus rejected, crucified, dying at the hands of those He had come to save. And then it all made sense.

The strange thing, and yet the wonderful thing, is that even though Jesus died on a cross, apparently defeated, forsaken even by His own disciples, yet His death attracted more followers than His life ever had!

And still that isn't surprising. Because when the tomb couldn't hold Him, when He walked out of it the Conqueror over death, men began to realize who He was. They began to realize that they had crucified the Son of God. And they began asking, "What shall we do?"

A man named Saul, a hater of Christians, saw a vision of Jesus on the way to Damascus. And immediately he asked, "What shall I do?"

Paul began preaching that Jesus was exactly who He said He was, the Son of God. And the jailer in Philippi asked, "What must I do to be saved?"

And men have been asking that question ever since.

Just what *do* we have to do to become a Christian? How *does* one accept Christ and become His follower? What is involved?

It's so easy to talk all around the subject when what you really want to know is *how*. And that was my concern as I told you my story. Now that I have told it simply and honestly let me review. Let me go over the steps once again so that we shall not forget.

So how does one become a Christian? How do you go about it? *First, you look!*

Jesus said through the prophet Isaiah, "Look to me and be saved." Isaiah 45:22, NEB.

And John the Baptist said of Jesus, "Look, the Lamb of God, who takes away the sin of the world!" John 1:29, NIV.

The apostle Paul said, "Let us fix our eyes on Jesus." Hebrews 12:2, NIV.

Pilate, the Roman ruler, didn't realize it. But he was preaching the gospel in capsule form—in just three words—when he said, "Behold the man!" John 19:5.

And what do we see when we look? Just a good man? A great teacher? A political reformer? An actor? A martyr?

No. We are looking at a man who claimed to be the Son of God. And either He was who He said He was, or He lied. And a liar is not a good man. So it is impossible for Jesus to be only a good man. He was who He said He was—or He was the greatest impostor the world has ever known!

We are looking at the Man who came to show us what God is like. We see Him passing through villages and healing all the sick. Loving His way into every heart that was willing to be loved. Setting free the captives of sin. A strong Man who never compromised, but who had tears in His voice as He spoke His scathing rebukes to the arrogant and the proud.

We see the Man who was born to be crucified. The Man dying on a cross—the most despised instrument of death in His day. A martyr? No. A martyr could not touch our need. We are watching a sacrifice. We are watching God dying in our place, on a cross that should have been ours—so that we could live.

And what happens when we look? Jesus said, "I, if I be lifted up from the earth, will draw all men unto me." John 12:32.

Every man who looks at Jesus will be attracted, will be drawn—*if he does not resist.*

The mighty attraction of the cross—of God dying in our place—is enough to draw any man, to melt any proud heart.

But God uses no force. We can resist if we choose.

Pilate looked at Jesus. He was attracted. He was drawn. He was convicted. He felt that the Man standing before him might actually be a divine being. He said, "I find no fault in him." John 19:4.

But Pilate resisted. And so he found no salvation in looking.

But the woman at the well looked—and found living water. Peter looked—and wept tears of repentance. Mary looked—and seven devils were gone. Paul looked—and served till his dying day the Man he had been persecuting.

When we look at Jesus, we are attracted to Him, we are drawn.

But you say, "What if He doesn't draw me? What if I'm not on His list?"

Don't worry. You're on His list. You will be drawn if you do not resist.

But there is more. The longer you look, the more your ideas of God are changed. No longer do you think of God as a tyrant waiting with a big stick to catch you in some wrong. Instead, as you watch, you see your own Creator loving you personally enough to die in your place. It's an incredible sacrifice—a sacrifice that could never happen. And yet it did. And somehow you know that it will take all eternity to understand it.

And the longer you look, the more your ideas of your own condition change. The more you realize how desperately you need that sacrifice—how utterly lost you are without it!

The longer you look, the more you are convicted of your need. The more your heart is broken. And the more it is healed!

But how do you accept the Lord Jesus as your Saviour? How do you accept the sacrifice? How do you tell Him you want the alienation to be healed? It must be difficult, you say.

No, it isn't.

You see, so often we think of God as being way up there, and us way down here. And we think there must be a long, hard ladder to climb. But that isn't the way it is at all. Our Lord is anxious to heal the separation—so anxious that He has traveled the distance. He stands just outside the door of your heart. And He says, "Here I am! I stand at the door and knock. If anyone hears my voice and opens the door, I will go in and eat with him, and he with me." Revelation 3:20, NIV.

Why doesn't He come in? Because He will not enter uninvited. He will not force the will. He waits for your invitation. But that's all it takes to accept Him as your Saviour. Just invite Him in.

You say, "Surely it can't be that simple. Surely there are things we have to do. There must be steps we have to take."

Yes, other steps will follow the first. And we'll be talking about them. But they will be motivated, every one of them, by what you see on that cross outside Jerusalem. Every step you take in the Christian life will be powered by the fascination of the Man loving you to the death when you didn't love Him at all—and when you were driving the nails!

You? Driving the nails? Me? Driving the nails?

Yes, it's easy to blame Judas for what happened on Calvary. It's easy to blame Pilate—or the Roman soldiers. But if we keep looking at that cross, eventually will come the realization that we did it, that our fingerprints are on those nails!

And nothing else will so change us, so transform us—nothing else will so fire our love and power our witness—as that realization. Nothing else will so cut our hearts to the quick. And nothing else will so heal!

Has It Come to That?

There is an old story, somewhat lacking in authenticity, about a man chasing a rabbit through the woods. He was almost upon the rabbit, the story says, when suddenly they came to the edge of a cliff. The rabbit, of course, had the advantage. It was small and agile, able to make a quick turn and avoid going over the precipice. But the man couldn't make the turn and went over.

As he was falling, he sighted a limb on a bush and was able to grab it. Then he began to scream for help. He shouted, "Is anyone up there?" There was no answer. So he yelled again, this time still louder, "Is anyone up there?"

Finally he heard a stately voice from somewhere above, "To whom do you wish to speak?"

And the man, desperate as he hung onto the limb, managed to shout, "Anyone who will help me."

Then, according to the legend, the strange interchange continued. The voice from above asked, "Do you have faith?" And the man replied, "Yes." He hoped it was true.

"All right," said the voice, "if you have faith, let go of that limb."

The man hesitated. He looked down. It was a long way down. All that stood between him and certain death, it seemed, was that limb. Finally, after a long silence, the desperate man shouted, "Is anyone *else* up there?"

Just a story. Just a legend. But how true to life. We think we have faith in God. We talk about it, and boast about it. And we

193

get along fine—so long as our faith isn't challenged. But when it is—when we get into a tight spot where we have to throw our full weight on it, where we have to demonstrate it or deny it— that's another story.

It isn't easy to let go the limb we're holding onto—no matter how insecure it may be—and just trust God. And many a man, when God has asked of him a full surrender, has looked around for some other god to worship, for a faith that didn't require that kind of commitment. It isn't easy to let go!

One Christian was telling another about how all his efforts to resolve a certain problem had failed. And he concluded, "There is literally nothing left for me to do now but to trust the Lord."

His friend replied sympathetically, "Has it come to *that?*"

Has it come to that? Must we surrender? Must we actually turn the management of our lives over to our Lord? Why can't we just say we believe? Why do we have to demonstrate it by letting go?

Surrender is the most difficult thing in the Christian life. Yet surrender is the only key, the only entrance, to a saving relationship with our Lord. How can He save us until we stop trying to save ourselves? How can He save us until we are willing to let Him save us His way?

Surrender sounds like risk. That's why we fear it. We seem to think that God is just waiting to dump a whole assortment of unpleasant things on our heads the moment we surrender. Surely He will ask us to give up everything we don't want to give up, and do everything we don't want to do, and experience everything we don't want to experience.

What kind of God do we think He is? Would a God who loves us enough to give His only Son to die for us—would He go out of His way to make life as unpleasant as He could? The apostle Paul asks it this way: "He that spared not his own Son, but delivered him up for us all, how shall he not with him also freely give us all things?" Romans 8:32.

Listen. If you knew Him, if you really knew Him, you would be eager to let Him manage your life. You would know that it's perfectly safe. You would know that it involves no risk at all. Rather, the deeper your commitment, the more complete your surrender, the greater will be the sense of wonder at His love, His providence, His unfailing care. When you surrender to the Lord Jesus Christ, you are surrendering to One who loves you as if you were the only person in the world to love. Could there be any risk in that?

And yet surrender, for a proud heart, is very, very difficult!

Bertrand Russell, referring to the pride of the intellectual, once wrote, "Every man would like to be God, if it were possible; some few find it difficult to admit the impossibility."

Human nature finds it hard to surrender the driver's seat—hard to move over and let God do the driving. But how else can He ever do for us what we can't do for ourselves?

How do we make that surrender? How do we enter into that saving relationship with our Lord? To make it very, very simple, let me answer that question with three short, crisp sentences: 1. I am a sinner. 2. I can't do it. 3. But God can.

First—*I am a sinner*. There is nothing more difficult for a proud heart than to acknowledge—not weakness, not a personality problem, but *sin*. We have to call sin by its right name. We have to quit blaming our heredity and our environment and everything else we find to blame, and come to the place where we say, "I'm to blame. No one else is responsible. God help me!"

And then to the second painful fact: *I can't do it*. I can no more save myself than I can turn the waters of Niagara and send them roaring *up* the falls. I can't manufacture personal victory. I can't buy it in a bottle—or discover it in any formula. I can't bring it about by self-discipline. Every human attempt to tame the tiger within will only lead to disappointment. Victory is a gift of the Lord Jesus Christ. Victory is a miracle.

I am a sinner. I can't do it. And number 3. *But God can!*

A man will never find personal victory until he throws aside his miserable crutches and says, "Lord, I am a sinner. I've made a mess out of my life. I can't manage it. I bring my defeated life to You just as a child brings a stubborn toy to his father. You make it work. I can't. *But You can!*"

That's how simple it is. It's difficult only because it isn't easy for a proud, hard heart to be broken. It isn't easy for a man to surrender, to admit that he is weak. But surrender is the key.

Without surrender there is no miracle, no victory, only continual defeat.

Surrender happens when we look at Calvary and see Jesus dying there in our place, on a cross that should have been ours. Surrender happens when that cross becomes more important than our pride, when we know that we don't want to wound the Saviour again—ever!

Then the miracle happens!

Pride Turns Itself In

The Salem witchcraft trials of 1692 splashed a blot on American history. But what happened afterward makes you proud to be an American!

Today only a gaunt oak tree marks Gallows Hill, the spot where twenty innocent victims, during three months of trials in 1692, were executed as witches and buried without ceremony in common graves.

It was a time of hysteria in Salem, Massachusetts. Satan himself seemed to have descended upon the town. At least a good many people were accused of being in league with him. Something like a hundred and fifty people were said to be witches and were tried in court. Scores were imprisoned. Twenty were executed. Salem was determined to be free of witches!

It all started when a number of teen-age girls were caught playing forbidden games of magic. This, in the Puritan atmosphere of those days, was considered very serious. So when they were discovered, the girls panicked. They screamed, they trembled, and threw themselves to the ground.

When they saw that their elders were much impressed by their strange behavior, the quick-thinking youngsters decided they had a good act going. So they continued it. Here was a way to escape punishment.

The doctor was called. He said he couldn't do anything for them. The ministers were called. And the ministers said that the girls were bewitched.

The misbehaving teen-agers continued their act. If they were bewitched, someone must be bewitching them. So they began to accuse various members of the community. The older people, of course, were their targets.

The youngsters proved their charges, at least to the satisfaction of their elders, by falling into fits and writhing on the floor whenever the accused person touched them or even looked at them.

And so the hysteria grew. Suspicion was in the air. There were more and more accusations. There were court trials. There were excommunications. There were hangings!

So it was in 1692. But as the hysteria died down, the Puritan conscience began to work. The people of Salem began to see what they had done. They saw that innocent people had been put to death at their hands. Salem repented!

And Salem knew that true repentance leads to the confession of guilt!

Just five years after the tragic hysteria, Samuel Sewall, one of the judges of the witchcraft trials, and who later became chief justice, made a public apology. He stood humbly at his pew in the church while the minister read his confession. He said he desired "to take the blame and shame of it, asking pardon of men, and especially desiring prayers that God, who has an unlimited authority, would pardon that sin."

Think of it! A public confession from a judge. But that wasn't all. The jurors published a confession signed by all twelve men, saying they feared they had been guilty of innocent blood.

The minister, Samuel Parris, issued a statement expressing his repentance and asking pardon. But even that did not satisfy the members of his church. He was dismissed from his post.

Chief justice of the witchcraft court was William Stoughton, who had been a strong supporter of the trials. But it was he who, as acting governor, signed a declaration setting aside a day of fasting for the community to express repentance for the witchcraft wrongs.

Anne Putman, the ringleader of the girls who had made the accusations, made a public confession. She said she had accused persons she now believed to be innocent. And she said, "I desire to lie in the dust and to be humbled for it in that I was a cause, with others, of so sad a calamity to them and their families."

Salem was as caught up in repentance as it had been in the campaign against supposed witchcraft. Excommunications were reversed, property restored, names cleared, a monument erected to the memory of Rebecca Nurse, one of those who was hanged. Every group in the community made some gesture of apology—even witnesses and bystanders.

Evidently Salem's repentance was deep and genuine. It made its confession public because its sin had been public. And it did everything possible to undo its wrong. True repentance will never do less.

I ask you, Where in all history is there a record of such genuine and unanimous repentance—unless it be when the entire city of Nineveh repented at the preaching of Jonah?

Yes, America can be proud of Salem, after all!

Confession is a great and noble thing. It isn't easy. Guilt always prefers to remain hidden. It balks at turning itself in. It takes real courage to stand up and say "I was wrong." But how many things might be different, how many wounds healed, how many names cleared, how many lives made happy—if, in private and public life, we had more of such greatness!

A silent sense of guilt is not enough. A silent sorrow is not enough. Says the apostle John, "*If we confess* our sins, he is faithful and just to forgive us our sins, and to cleanse us from all unrighteousness." 1 John 1:9.

Confession must precede forgiveness. It must precede cleansing. There's no other way. If our sin is against God alone, we may confess to God alone. But if our sin has wounded another, we must confess to that other. And if our sin has been public, our confession must be public. Our confession must be as wide as our sin.

It's a strange and phony repentance that does not lead a man to say, "I was wrong"—or "God be merciful to me a sinner."

But too often repentance, even when it calls itself by that name, is shallow and hypocritical. Guilt, squeezed into a corner, mumbles, "I guess I goofed"—and slips away as fast as it can.

Confession, even when it is made, too often is transparently synthetic. It's plastic. It isn't real. It is so loaded down with qualifications and excuses and reservations and reasons-why-I-did-it that it is meaningless.

We recoil when we see in others this endless cycle of self-justification, all the while pretending perfection. We recognize it as the height of hypocrisy. But how many of us practice it ourselves?

Guilt finds so many ways of avoiding full exposure, full responsibility, full acceptance of blame. We shy away from getting down on our knees and saying, "Lord, I'm to blame. Me. Not somebody else."

We blame it to our childhood, to Dad's bank account or lack of it, to which side of the tracks we grew up on, to a teacher we had in kindergarten, to something somebody said to us, or did to us, that we can't even remember. Anything but take the blame ourselves.

Or we get caught up with the popular idea that all we need is to forgive ourselves. When will we learn that guilt is not something we can manage ourselves? Forgiveness is not something we can manage ourselves. The healing must come from outside. Only God is equipped to handle it. And even He can't heal a guilt that we won't admit.

Confession is a battle with pride. And pride doesn't want to turn itself in. Pride says, "If I confess my sin, what will it do to my reputation?" Confession means telling another—or a group of others—that you are not perfect—that something is wrong with *you*. And pride balks at that.

You see, sin is a strictly personal thing. There is no such thing as sin apart from a person. A star or a mountain or a city hall cannot sin. Only people sin. No laboratory in the world can isolate the essence of sin and put it in a test tube. So when a man confesses his sin—and calls it that—he's not confessing something in the environment, or something in a test tube that he can hold up and condemn. He is confessing something within himself. And that's hard to do.

So pride waits. And waits. Pride doesn't want to trade in its reputation, its self-centered ambition, its self-justification and pretense—even for cleansing and peace and a new life.

But friend, it's a terrible thing to be too proud to repent, too proud to say, "I was wrong." It's a tragic thing to wait so long, to go so far, that there is no way back, to ignore the call until you can't hear it anymore, to let the heart get so hard that even the Spirit of God can't break it anymore. For remember, only broken hearts ever repent—and turn themselves in.

And only broken hearts are healed.

The Missing Chapter

Have you ever felt like a book with a missing chapter? Something that ought to be there but isn't? Have you stretched the horizons of your life to the limit—and felt there ought to be something more?

Maybe you're right. And maybe there is.

Classics in religious books are few and far between. Not many are enduring enough to achieve that status. But I have one in my library that I prize very much. It was written in the last century by a Quaker named Hannah Whitall Smith. And it's called *The Christian's Secret of a Happy Life*. My 1952 edition says that two million copies had then been sold. It's still selling.

But imagine my surprise to discover recently that my copy of the book is not all there. A chapter is missing!

I owe this discovery to the late Catherine Marshall, wife of the famed Peter Marshall. She, of course, was an author in her own right.

Catherine Marshall, too, prized this book for many years. But in 1970 someone gave her a very old copy of the book—an 1885 edition. And as she paged through it, she was surprised to find that it contained a chapter that has been deleted from later editions. It was a chapter about the Holy Spirit.

Why had the publishers left it out? What was wrong with it? Naturally she was curious. And when she had read the chapter, she was even more curious.

She found nothing dangerous or extreme or unorthodox in

the chapter. There's nothing unorthodox about a belief in the Holy Spirit, for the Holy Spirit is the Third Person of the Godhead—just as truly God as the Father and the Son. And there's nothing wrong with the desire to be filled with the Spirit, baptized with the Spirit, for that's Scripture too.

Hannah Smith's chapter was filled with Scripture and with common sense. She said the baptism of the Spirit should not be thought of as a single experience but as a life. She warned that the "baptism means far more than emotion. It means to be immersed or dipped into the Spirit of God, into His character and nature. The real evidence of one's baptism is neither emotion nor any single gift such as tongues, rather that there *must* be Christ-likeness in life and character: by fruits in the life we shall know whether or not we have the Spirit."

She wasn't ruling out emotion, you understand. She said that the baptism of the Spirit can be, though it isn't always, a very emotional and overwhelming sense of His presence.

What could be wrong with such a sensible and balanced presentation as that? Catherine Marshall was now determined to find out why the publishers had felt it necessary to delete it. And she turned up a very interesting story!

It seems that in 1865 "Hannah and her husband, Robert Pearsall Smith, and their children moved to the village of Milltown, New Jersey, where Robert took charge of a branch of the family glass business. There Hannah met a group called 'the Holiness Methodists.' "

Some of the most penetrating and valuable parts of *The Christian's Secret of a Happy Life*, the book she was later to write, were to come from insights she gained from this group. She was able to translate their teachings from their distinctive language into everyday words we could all understand.

Catherine Marshall found that "eventually Robert Smith was as caught up as his wife in all this. One summer the Smiths went to a ten-day Holiness Camp Meeting at a woodland campsite along the New Jersey coast. The purpose of these meetings, in Hannah's words, was 'to open our hearts to the teachings of the Holy Spirit and His coming into seekers' hearts.' But it was Robert rather than his wife who received an extraordinary emotional experience."

Hannah later told what happened. She said, "After the meeting my husband had gone alone into a spot in the woods to continue to pray by himself. Suddenly, from head to foot he was shaken with what seemed like a magnetic thrill of heavenly delight, and floods of glory seemed to pour through him, soul and body, with the inward assurance that was the longed-for baptism of the Holy Spirit."

She said, "The whole world seemed transformed for him, every leaf and blade of grass quivered with exquisite colour. . . . Everybody looked beautiful to him, for he seemed to see the Divine Spirit within each one. . . . This ecstasy lasted for several weeks, and was the beginning of a wonderful career of spiritual power and blessing."

Naturally this made Hannah desire a similar experience. She went to the altar night after night. She prayed for hours on end. But nothing happened. Not then or ever did she have an emotional experience such as had come to her husband.

At first she was disappointed. Then she realized that God had already given her a revelation of His character that had changed her life. She had wanted emotion. But God had given her fact—something more permanent and substantial.

But the story isn't over. In 1873 the Smiths moved to England, where their lives were intertwined, by marriage or by friendship, with such names as Bertrand Russell, George Bernard Shaw, and others of the elite of England. For years the Smiths conducted a very successful lay ministry among the aristocracy.

And then in the spring of 1875 Robert Smith traveled to Germany, where he held highly successful evangelistic and teaching meetings before large crowds, always in a highly charged emotional atmosphere. In a letter to his wife he exulted, "All Europe is at my feet!" When engraved pictures of him were offered for sale, eight thousand sold immediately.

Catherine Marshall's narration continues: "Then the blow fell. Gossip began about Robert Pearsall Smith's improper conduct with female admirers. No one then or now knows the exact truth of the matter. The emotionalism so appealing to Smith had apparently gotten out of hand.

"The rumors got into the press. Meetings scheduled in England were canceled by their sponsors, and for a time the Smiths returned to New Jersey. Hannah quietly stood by her husband. She wrote a friend of . . . the 'crushing blow' that had befallen Robert.

"And crush him it did. He gave way to discouragement, disillusionment, and to a degree of cynicism. Robert sank into a joyless old age, while Hannah went on from strength to strength, her quiet deep faith carrying her triumphantly over all sorts of trials and difficulties."

Said Catherine Marshall, "In Robert Smith's case, tragedy resulted when he succumbed to the temptation to idolize emotion instead of worshiping Jesus." With Hannah Smith, no ecstasy was apparent. Rather, she had a quiet, happy confidence as a result of her balanced convictions about God.

"As for the missing chapter," said Catherine Marshall, "clearly editors had been afraid of the subject. It was fire. Hadn't Robert Smith been burned? Safer to omit it, they must have concluded."

And then she made a very significant comment. She said, "As Len and I pondered Hannah's story [Len was her last husband], we agreed that the modern surge of the Spirit in America may stand poised at the edge of this same problem—too great a love affair with emotion, too little grounding in Scripture, too wanting in garden-variety discipline, too small an emphasis on purity, strict honesty, morality—Christ's own life living in us."

Could anyone have said it better? I've been quoting from Catherine Marshall's book *Something More.*

The present love affair with emotion is no surprise. It isn't difficult to understand it. Conservative religion, at least too much of it, has been smothered under a blanket of cold, lifeless formality for so long—it just had to get some air! It had to breathe!

Religion that doesn't breathe isn't going to reach very many people. This generation is tired of being suffocated.

On the other hand, if people ask only "How does it feel?" and never "How does it check with Scripture?" aren't they on dangerous ground? Hasn't the pendulum swung a little too far?

Aren't we on dangerous ground when we try to measure the genuineness of our conversion, or of our continuing walk with Christ, by the amount of emotion accompanying it? Shouldn't we see a red light flashing when we begin to focus our eyes more on emotion than on the Saviour? Shouldn't we see a red light when we make feeling the goal instead of the by-product—when we make it an end in itself?

There is nothing wrong with emotion. But emotion needs intelligent control. It needs discipline. A man who has had an experience with the Lord Jesus Christ ought to be different from what he was before. And if he isn't, if his life style is still the same, his experience ought to be suspect.

Does the experience change the life, or only the mood? That's the question. Does it change a man? Or does it merely deceive him into thinking he doesn't need changing? That's the danger.

Emotion is not the big thing in life. Living counts too—everyday living. And the red light ought to flash frantically when we try to substitute emotion for a reformation in the life.

Too many so-called conversions and too many so-called baptisms of the Spirit leave men and women just as they were before, their life styles and their habits unchanged. And it ought not to be that way.

Listen. Not many years ago, in the city of Oakland, California, 21,600 decisions for Christ were registered during a large evangelistic crusade. But about a third of those 21,600—that would be about 7,200 people—gave false names and addresses on the decision cards they filled out.

I ask you, How much is a decision worth—how solid is it, how sincere is it—when a person deliberately lies while he is filling out his decision card?

The ministry of Jesus was a sensational ministry—in the best sense of the word. It was the most sensational ministry the world has ever seen. But it was not a ministry of wind and fire and earthquake. And it was not show business. Never once did Jesus say to the people, "Come tomorrow and I'll show you that I can walk on water." Or "Come tomorrow and I'll show you that I can feed five thousand of you with a little boy's lunch."

And yet He had the power of the Spirit as no other ever had it, or ever will. John the Baptist said of Jesus, "To him God gives the Spirit without limit." John 3:34, NIV.

Jesus told us something of what the work of the spirit would be in our lives. He said, "When he, the Spirit of truth, comes, he will guide you into all truth." John 16:13, NIV.

Notice that He did not say, "When the Spirit comes, you will know that you *have received* all truth." No. He said, "He will guide you *into* all truth." There is still truth to be learned, to be received into the life.

Unfortunately, there are some who feel that a strong emotional experience means that they have arrived at all truth, that there is nowhere else to go. They aren't interested in truth anymore, once they have received an emotional experience. They want to stop right there and forget about truth. But that's dangerous!

Listen! God will never give us an experience that makes the Bible unnecessary.

And the Spirit of God—this is important—will never give us a revelation that in any way contradicts His Written Word. The Spirit of God does not contradict Himself. Any time we get a personal revelation that is contrary to the Bible, we'd better check quick to see what spirit it is. It won't be the Spirit of God!

The apostle John said, "Do not believe every spirit, but test the spirits to see whether they are from God." 1 John 4:1, NIV.

Pretty good advice, isn't it?

Jesus said of the Spirit, "He, when He comes, will convict the world concerning sin." John 16:8, NASB.

The work of the Spirit is to convict us of sin, to convince us of our need of a Saviour.

So if a spirit tells you that you're OK, that you don't need anything, that you've arrived—is that the Spirit of God? Never!

Catherine Marshall prayed for the Spirit. And what happened? She said, "The first discipline He gave me was a leash for my tongue. For others the Spirit may give torrents of ecstatic speech. I needed the discipline of not speaking the careless or negative or discouraging word. For weeks I was put through the sharp training of opening my mouth to speak and hearing from the Teacher 'Stop! No, don't say it. Close the mouth.' "

When we make a full surrender to the Spirit of God, He will give us what we need—not necessarily what we think we need. It's that full surrender, that complete surrender, that is all important. And that surrender, that commitment, must include a willingness to obey Him. For we read in the book of Acts, "We are witnesses of these things, and so is the Holy Spirit, whom God has given *to those who obey him.*" Acts 5:32, NIV.

Can we expect to be filled with the Spirit and go on disobeying Him? Hardly!

One more caution. Satan, the enemy of God, stands ready to counterfeit every gift of the Spirit. And he's able to do it. He will one day counterfeit the coming of Christ Himself. And if he's able to attempt that, won't he attempt to counterfeit the gifts of the Spirit? It is no trick at all for Satan to counterfeit the gift of prophecy, or the gift of teaching, or the gift of healing, or the gift of tongues. After all, he is an angel fallen. He can easily speak any language on earth.

Am I condemning any of the gifts? No. Not one of them. God gave them at Pentecost. He will give them again whenever He chooses, and as He chooses. I'm only saying that there is a Holy Spirit and an unholy spirit. I'm only saying, Watch out for counterfeits. Keep your eyes open—and your Bible close by!

But now, with those cautions, let me say this. For most of us the filling of the Holy Spirit is the one great need of our lives. It is the missing chapter—a chapter that needs to be restored, a chapter we dare not leave out. Too many of us are going along satisfied with a humdrum experience that doesn't mean a thing. God wants us to have more. So much more!

We ought to be praying for the Spirit as we've never prayed for anything in our lives. We ought to be getting closer to our Lord than we've ever been before.

And then we ought to let the Spirit decide what gift to give us. Don't you think? God isn't a Santa Claus who needs a list from us. He knows what gift you can use best. He knows what gift fits me best. Let's let Him choose.

Let's let Him come into our lives in any way He chooses. He

may not come with wind or fire or a blinding light or other tongues. He may come with conviction, with new truth, with a leash for our tongues. But, thank God, He will come with a power over sin that we have never known. And that's what we need above all else. That's what the filling of the Spirit is all about.

And it doesn't have to be a missing chapter!

How to Live With a Tiger

For some reason we've had the idea that when a man becomes a Christian, the tiger politely takes his leave and that's the end of the conflict. The man has accepted Christ. He has made his decision. His mind is made up. He isn't torn between two anymore.

Once we become Christians we won't sin anymore. We won't be tempted anymore—at least not very much. And certainly we'll never lose our temper again. So we reason.

And then suddenly, without warning, it happens. The tiger scores again. And down we go—as far down as we were up. And we wonder if we were ever converted at all!

The truth is that, strange as it may seem, incredible as it may seem, there is more conflict in the life of the Christian than in the life of the non-Christian. Let me say it another way. There is more conflict in a man after conversion than there was before conversion.

Are you surprised? Yes, the man who accepts Christ can expect more conflict than before. He can expect to be tempted more. And he can expect to be plunged into despondency and despair—and be thoroughly confused—until he understands what is going on.

It's simply this. The man without Christ has only one nature—the nature with which he was born. And that nature sins just as easily as water runs downhill. There is nothing to oppose it. There is no conflict.

But the man who has committed his life to Christ, who has

211

submitted to the miracle of conversion, has a new life within, a new nature. And that new nature is in continual opposition to the old.

You see now why life may seem to run along so smoothly for the unconverted man. He has only one nature—and its control is unopposed. But not long after conversion, just when he thinks the old nature is dead and gone, he discovers that a conflict is going on within him.

He has two natures now. And the two are in conflict. True, he has the new nature that Christ gave him. But the old nature, the tiger nature, doesn't want to die. So the two are going to battle it out!

God doesn't suddenly destroy the tiger. He doesn't lift us above being tempted. He doesn't remove our power to choose. He places within the converted man a new nature that is able to overcome the old. But whether it does or not is up to the man himself.

No wonder there is tension and conflict in the life of the new Christian. He has two natures. And they don't like each other.

The apostle Paul understood this conflict. He experienced it himself. And this is what he says about it: "Here is my advice. Live your whole life in the Spirit and you will not satisfy the desires of your lower nature. For the whole energy of the lower nature is set against the Spirit, while the whole power of the Spirit is contrary to the lower nature. Here is the conflict, and that is why you are not able to do what you want to do." Galatians 5:16, 17, Phillips.

Two natures locked in conflict. That's why a Christian sometimes finds himself doing things he doesn't really want to do.

But does this mean that he is doomed to forever live with a civil war inside? No, it doesn't. One nature or the other will win out. One nature or the other will gain control. One nature or the other will die.

And now listen. Which nature eventually wins could depend on which nature rules your life *tomorrow*. And would you like me to tell you which nature will rule in *your* life tomorrow? Would you?

You say, "Pastor Vandeman, you don't know me!"

I'm not so sure. Listen carefully. I may not know you personally, but I do know this: The nature that will rule your life tomorrow will be the nature that is the stronger tomorrow. If the new nature is stronger, it will rule. If the old nature is stronger, it will rule. Every day of your life it will be that way. The nature that is stronger at that moment will rule.

And so, without knowing you personally at all, I can also predict that whichever nature is stronger when Jesus Christ returns to this earth, or when you come to the end of the way, will determine your eternal destiny. For in that day your standing before God, and my standing before God, will depend simply upon which nature has gained control of our lives—the old or the new. And it will be one or the other. I cannot be both!

And now I want to share with you a priceless secret. *Whichever nature you feed* will be the stronger. Whichever one you feed will survive. The other will die.

You see, the miracle of conversion, the miracle of the new birth—that's God's part. That's His work. There is absolutely nothing you or I can do to bring it about—except to open the floodgates and invite the Saviour in. He will implant the new life. That's His part. And then our part is to feed it. And if we feed it, it will be the stronger.

Now, I don't mean for a moment that God simply works a miracle at the beginning, at conversion, and then leaves us on our own to battle the tiger in our own strength. No. The Christian life is a miracle all the way through. His power is constantly available to us. I'm simply saying that there is something we must do. We must feed the new nature.

But this is the secret that so many have not understood. This is why so many have become discouraged. This is why so many earnest, sincere people feel frustrated. This is why so many, years after to their commitment to Christ, still have a civil war going on inside—when the old nature should have died long ago.

Why didn't it? What happened? Simply this: Instead of feeding the new nature and letting the old nature die from lack of attention, they have been feeding both natures just enough to keep them both alive!

And that's an unhappy situation. Is it any wonder they are miserable? They have just enough of Christ in the life to produce conflict—but not enough to produce control. Just enough of Christ in the life to make living in tune with a rebel world embarrassing. And just enough of that rebel world in the life to make living with Christ uncomfortable.

Let me illustrate it this way. Suppose that out in the mountains two wild animals are fighting each other. Looking on, you don't know which one will win. Both seem equally strong. They seem evenly matched.

But now let us say that one of them is drawn away from the area of conflict for a time—perhaps caught or trapped somewhere—and for several weeks he is without food. He starves while the other eats well.

And now in that condition—one starving and one well-fed— suppose they meet in combat again. Tell me. Which one will win?

Is there any question? You know which one will win. It's the one which has been fed.

You say, "How do you feed the new nature?"

Well, the health habits of the new life are much like those of the body. If we want the body to live, we let it breathe, don't we? If we want it to be healthy, we feed it. If we want it to be strong, we give it plenty of exercise. And it's the same with the new life.

Prayer is the life-giving oxygen that sustains the new nature. It is the breath of the soul. Without it, death soon follows.

So let the new nature breathe. And then feed it. And you know where to find that food. It's in the Word of God. For "man shall not live by bread alone, but by every word that proceedeth out of the mouth of God." Matthew 4:4.

So take the Book—God's Book. Take it in the early morning, before the tensions of the day begin. Let its message refresh you. Let it link you with the heart of God.

As Columbus skirted the shores of the New World, the ship sailed into fresh water. They were in the mouth of the River Orinoco. But they didn't know.

It was suggested that they might be approaching an island.

But said the famed discoverer, "No such river flows from an island. That mighty torrent must drain the waters of a continent."

Just so, the more you personally read the Book of God, permitting it to speak to your mind and heart, the more you will know that it does not come from the empty hearts of impostors, but that it springs from the depths of eternal love and wisdom.

That mighty torrent will pour into your soul the fresh life-blood of the new nature—if you will let it.

And then, the only way to keep what you receive is to share it with somebody else.

A doctor once found a little dog with a broken leg by the roadside. He took the little fellow home, cleaned him up, set the broken bone, and put a little splint on it to hold it in place.

The little dog loved the doctor. He followed the kind man around the house and around the yard—until the leg was well. Then suddenly he disappeared. "That's gratitude," thought the doctor. "As long as he needed me, he stayed. As soon as he didn't need me, he ran away."

But the doctor spoke too soon. For the very next day there was a scratching at the back door, and there was the little dog. Back again, wagging his tail. But beside him was another little dog. And that other little dog was lame!

Yes, that's the way the new life grows. You can't keep it to yourself. It must be shared.

Prayer—Bible study—sharing. These feed the new nature. And remember. The nature you feed is the nature that will win.

Our part, you see, is to open the floodgates to the power of the living Christ. Our part—by prayer and Bible study and sharing—is to open the door for Christ to work in our lives. These make it possible for Him to continue the work He has begun. These give Him the opportunity to sustain the new life that He has implanted in us. These are the ways we invite Him, each day, to do for us what we can't do for ourselves!

The tiger inside, the nature with which we were born, is too much for us to face alone. We've seen it demonstrated again and again. There is only one person who can conquer the tiger in your life or mine. It's Jesus, the Lamb of God.

A lamb stronger than a tiger? Yes, that's the beautiful paradox of what God is waiting to do in your life. For remember—there is only one throne in your heart. Only one can occupy it. And so long as Jesus the Lamb of God rules your life—at your invitation—the tiger hasn't a chance!

Hope for Repeaters

If I were to mention an army that has become expert at surprise, at night fighting, and at tricking the enemy, you would probably think I have in mind a certain Middle Eastern army that has often achieved brilliant success with such strategy.

True.

But there is another army—one of far greater concern to you and me. It's an invisible army, an army made up of uncounted angels—fallen angels, angels banished from heaven along with their leader. And every one of these angels-turned-demons is a brilliant strategist. Every one of them is an expert at surprise, at under-cover fighting, and at trickery. Their operations are not crude and clumsy. They are incredibly sophisticated—and incredibly subtle!

Their target? You. Your mind. Your will. Your conscience. Your destiny. Putting it bluntly, they are out to destroy you!

And do they politely leave when you become a Christian? No. They double their efforts. And remember. Their attacks come unannounced, just when you least expect them. They work under cover, often in disguise. We read of their leader, "Satan himself is transformed into an angel of light." 2 Corinthians 11:14.

They will trick you at every turn—if you let them. And they don't stop with tricks. They specialize in the supernatural—in miracles. The apostle John speaks of "spirits of devils, working miracles." Revelation 16:14.

So do you see what we face—every one of us?

217

But here's good news. You don't have to sin. Sin requires the consent of the individual. And that consent you don't have to give. The tempter can try to trick you. He can harass you. He can hound your steps like a shadow. But he cannot contaminate you against your will. There is no power under heaven that can force you to sin—without your consent.

And here's more good news: Temptation is not sin.

The familiar switchboard illustration will help us to understand. Let's say that in the switchboard of every heart there are two main trunk lines—Christ's line and the devil's line. But no matter how frequent or insistent or excited the flash of the enemy's light, it cannot contaminate you unless you make contact. You don't have to answer the light. You can just let it flash. The light is the temptation. Answering it is the sin.

And here's still more good news: God does not tempt us. The devil does. But God is in control. No temptation can come to us without God's permission. And did you know that every temptation is weighed and measured—to be sure it isn't too much for us—before God permits it to come our way? Listen: "No temptation has seized you except what is common to man. And God is faithful; he will not let you be tempted beyond what you can bear. But when you are tempted, he will also provide a way out so that you can stand up under it." 1 Corinthians 10:13, NIV.

And what is the way out? Who is the way out? It's Jesus. The answer to the problem of temptation is to let Jesus meet it for you. Don't try to take on Satan yourself. That's too big a job for any man. Let Jesus handle it. He is able. "You, dear children, are from God and have overcome them [evil spirits], because the one who is in you is greater than the one who is in the world." 1 John 4:4, NIV.

Jesus is able. God "is able to keep you from falling and to present you before his glorious presence without fault and with great joy." Jude 24, NIV.

Let Jesus handle every temptation that comes your way. To tackle the enemy on your own is to invite defeat.

A little girl explained how it works. She said, "When I see Satan coming, I say, 'Jesus, You go to the door.' So Jesus goes to the door. And when Satan sees Jesus, he says, 'Excuse me. I've come to the wrong house!' "

That's how simple it is.

But you say, "It can't be that easy. Isn't the Christian life hard? Isn't it supposed to be a struggle against sin?"

Yes, the Christian life is a battle and a march. God never intended us to sit back and do nothing.

You may be remembering the words of the apostle Paul: "In your struggle against sin, you have not yet resisted to the point of shedding your blood." Hebrews 12:4, NIV.

Let Jesus meet the temptation. That's easy. But struggle against sin, resist it—even to the point of shedding your blood. That's hard—very hard. Do we have a contradiction here? No.

Tell me. Who meets the temptation? Jesus. But who does the resisting? We do—because resisting is an act of the will. And our will is involved in every temptation—one way or the other. We decide how it shall be met, who is going to meet it. And the greatest struggles we have are in the mind, in the will.

You see, when Jesus goes to the door, all is well. But the battle you fight in your mind over whether to send Jesus to the door or go yourself—that struggle may be intense, it may be fierce!

And remember that even after Jesus has gone to the door, we still have our free choice. We can call Him back if we choose. We can say, "Wait a minute, Jesus. I want to talk to Satan myself." And believe me, when we do that we've had it!

So long as Jesus is in control of our lives, we are safe from the power of the enemy. So long as we let Him do the driving, we won't get off the road. Letting Him take the wheel is the answer to all the problems of Christian living. But at any moment you can change your mind and say, "Jesus, I guess I'll drive now." And He'll move over and let you drive. In the Christian life there is no force, no compulsion. You have the highest freedom. It's you who makes the decisions. And you make them in the mind, in the will.

Every battle with sin, every bout with temptation, is won or lost *first* in the mind. It's in the mind that we either resist temptation or toy with it. It's in the mind that we close the door on sin—or we rationalize that maybe this once, in this particular case, it will be all right after all. It's in the mind that we deceive ourselves.

The less we think about sin the better—because sin thrives on attention, even negative attention.

I keep remembering the Indian fakir who came to a village declaring he would demonstrate how to make gold. The villagers gathered around as he poured water into a huge caldron, put some coloring matter into it, and began to repeat magic words as he stirred.

When their attention was diverted for a moment, he let some gold nuggets slip down into the water. Stirring a little more, he poured off the water, and there was the gold at the bottom of the caldron.

The villagers' eyes bulged. The moneylender offered five hundred rupees for the formula, and the fakir sold it to him. "But," said the fakir, "you must not think of the red-faced monkey as you stir. If you do, the gold will never come!"

The moneylender promised to *remember* that he was to *forget*. But try as hard as he might, the red-faced monkey sat on the edge of his mind, spoiling all his gold.

Concentrating on your sins will get you into trouble. Keeping your eyes on Jesus will keep you out of it.

I think you see now why the enemy's target is the mind, the will. He knows what we must learn—that everything depends upon the action of the will. Satan knows that he cannot force us to sin. He can only try to trick us into *choosing* to sin. And so he turns all his guns against the will. He knows that anything that weakens the mind weakens the will—and weakens the conscience too, because the conscience operates through the mind. He cares not how he does it—with alcohol or drugs, with cigarettes or hypnosis, or even overeating or excessive fatigue. He knows that once the mind is breached, it is easier to breach it the second time. That's why hypnosis is so dangerous—because once the mind has been surrendered to another, once the locks are jimmied, the mind is never so strong again.

No wonder we are counseled to "guard your heart [your mind] more than any treasure." Proverbs 4:23, NEB.

Guard it carefully. Guard it diligently. Guard it at any cost!

But you say, "I have feelings that I can't control. I have desires and cravings that I can't control."

Yes, all of us have had that experience. Satan places unholy suggestions in every mind. But we don't have to make them welcome. We don't have to harbor them. We can *choose* not to follow his suggestions. We can *choose* not to be controlled by our cravings.

And here's the good news. God does not negotiate with your feelings or your cravings or your desires. He negotiates with the will. *The will is the real you.*

Everything depends upon the will. You can *choose* who your master will be. You can surrender your will to the Saviour. And does that make you a puppet? No. It makes you free. And Jesus said, "So if the Son sets you free, you will be free indeed." John 8:36, NIV.

And what happens to those feelings and desires that you can't control? God will take care of them in His own time and way. You will be free of them too!

Don't let the tempter bully you into thinking that you have to sin. Because you don't. The promise of God is that "sin shall not have dominion over you." Romans 6:14.

You don't have to sin! Satan cannot hold in his grasp one soul who desires to be free—and who chooses to be free.

But you say, "What if I fail? What if I fail over and over? Does that mean I was never converted—that I was never born again?"

Tell me. When a baby is born, does that mean he will never fall? And if he does fall—if he tumbles time after time—does that mean he was never born? Of course not!

Some of us haven't grown up yet. But that doesn't mean we haven't been born.

Says the apostle John, "I write this to you so that you will not sin. But if anybody does sin, we have one who speaks to the Father in our defense—Jesus Christ, the Righteous One. He is the atoning sacrifice for our sins." 1 John 2:1, 2, NIV.

A sacrifice has been provided. Forgiveness has been provided. And victory has been provided too. "Thanks be to God! He gives us the victory through our Lord Jesus Christ." 1 Corinthians 15:57, NIV.

Listen! There's hope for the repeater. There's hope for the defeated man. There's hope for the man or woman who feels like a chronic failure. There was hope for me—even when I shook my fist and tried to tell God I didn't want any hope.

And there's hope for you—whoever you are, wherever you are, whatever you are doing now, whatever your past life may have been. Jesus is willing to do for you what He did for me. And even more.

Think of it this way. It will give you courage. It will dissolve your despair. It will put a new spring in your step. You have failed. But *Jesus has not failed.*

Tell me. Have all the times that you have succeeded—have these added anything to *His* strength? No. And all the times you have failed—have these *detracted anything from* His strength? No. He is just as able to save you as before. You have failed. But Jesus has not failed. Get up and go right on.

Not so long ago the *Los Angeles Times* carried the story of a most unusual rescue operation. It took place 2400 feet above an airport—near the juncture of Yugoslavia, Austria, and Hungary.

A twenty-six-year-old skydiver—an experienced parachutist with 586 previous jumps to his credit—was stepping out the door of the plane when he tripped over some ropes. The ropes held his legs inside the plane, but allowed the rest of his body to fall out.

He could not climb back in. Nor could he get loose. And the pilot couldn't help. He was now alone in the cabin, and running low on fuel. He faced either running out of gas or trying to land with the skydiver hanging from the door.

Friends on the ground saw the predicament. One of them took off in a light plane with a hunting knife. He flew close to the plane in trouble and managed to pitch the knife to the parachutist, who caught it, cut the ropes around his legs, and dropped away. His parachute opened. He landed safely!

What a rescue!

You say, "That's just like me. That's my predicament. I'm caught in the ropes. I can't get in or out. And I haven't anything to cut the ropes!"

Yes, you have. The Lord Jesus, at tremendous risk to Himself, came to this planet to rescue you. He has tossed you a knife. And it's a sharp one. It's the Word of the living God—"sharper than any twoedged sword." Hebrews 4:12.

That Book is not only sharp. It is powerful. It's full of promises—promises that are meant for you personally. You can take them by faith, and they'll cut you loose. It's as simple as that.

There's just one catch. You have to *use* the knife. You have to *choose* to use it. Otherwise, what can God do?

But there's no power on earth that can keep you from dropping to your knees just now and making that happy choice—and falling free!